# JEWISH LAW
### and
# JEWISH LIFE

# JEWISH LAW

## BOOKS 2,3,4

Contracts
Real Estate
Sales
Usury

UNION OF AMERICAN HEBREW

# and JEWISH LIFE
## Selected Rabbinical Responsa

Compiled, Annotated, and Arranged by
JACOB BAZAK, *Professor*, Bar-Ilan University,
Judge, District Court, Jerusalem

Translated, Annotated, and Edited by
STEPHEN M. PASSAMANECK, *Professor of Rabbinics*,
Hebrew Union College-Jewish Institute of Religion
Los Angeles, California

CONGREGATIONS • NEW YORK

For our children
HAIM, ELI, MEIR, and TAMAR
·
DANIEL and EVE

*And they shall keep the way of the Lord: to do that which is right and just.*

Genesis 18:19

# CONTENTS FOR COMPLETE EDITION

## BOOK 2: Partnership, commercial practice, employer-employee relations, liability of an expert, the construction of a contract

## BOOK 3: Real property, landlord and tenant, responsibilities of neighbors, privacy

R. Joseph ibn Migash (No. 51)—An exchange of real property; defects in the property

R. Eliezer b. Nathan (No. 98)—A lease of a building, abandonment of the leased property due to persecution, an argument over the rent money

R. Isaac b. Sheshet Perfet (No. 510)—The lawful method of breaking a lease

R. Solomon b. Simon Duran (No. 439)—Sale of mortgaged property

R. Joseph ibn Migash (No. 132)—Joint responsibility of neighbors

R. Meir Halevi Abulafia (No. 272)—A wall between adjoining apartments

R. Solomon b. Adret (Sec. 4, No. 1143)—Tunneling under another's property; a right to use subsurface land

R. Solomon b. Adret (Sec. 1, No. 1144)—A window overlooking another's property

## BOOK 4: Sale of movables, sale of defective or damaged goods, usury, possession of movables

R. Meir b. Baruch of Rothenburg (No. 258)—A buyer's complaint: fraud or mistake of fact

R. Meir b. Baruch of Rothenburg (No. 809)—Confusion over a purchase price

R. Asher b. Yehiel (Sec. 97, No. 1)—Noncompliance with conditions concerning time and place of installment payments

R. Moses Maimonides (No. 275)—Sale of defective merchandise

R. Solomon b. Simon Duran (No. 476)—A garment sold and found to be damaged

R. Solomon b. Simon Duran (No. 16)—Usury

R. Solomon b. Simon Duran (No. 241)—Goods damaged in transit

R. Meir b. Baruch of Rothenburg (No. 251)—Property rescued from a fire

**BOOK 5: Creditor-debtor, surety, pledge, and promise to pay**

**BOOK 6: Communal regulation and enforcement, taxation**

*An early Jewish street scene.* (Hebrew Union College Skirball Museum, Los Angeles, Julie Breitstein, photographer)

# TRANSLATOR'S INTRODUCTION

THE TRANSLATION of Professor Jacob Bazak's anthology *Mishpat Vehalakhah* is a direct result of the Sixth World Congress of Jewish Studies, held in Jerusalem in August 1973. Professor Bazak and I gave papers at the same Jewish law session of the congress and discovered that we shared some mutual academic interests. Although we spent little time together, those minutes in Jerusalem prompted a voluminous correspondence and a fast friendship that led to this present work. The relationship that began in Jerusalem in 1973 has flourished to our mutual delight. Thus, if one purpose of such a congress is to bring people together to share ideas and launch cooperative efforts, this book is a genuine symbol of that purpose fulfilled.

Professor Bazak originally intended, through the publication of *Mishpat Vehalakhah*, to place samples of the rabbinic legal literature before the Israeli reading public, whether professional jurists, scholars, or laymen, in order to stimulate interest in and appreciation for this branch of Jewish scholarly literature. The material has endless treasures not only for legal scholarship but for several other fields; and there is no need to dilate upon the usefulness of responsa in scholarship, a usefulness which has been recognized for many years. But the responsa may have an even greater value for the nonscholarly reader who seeks absorption and stimulation. The audience beyond the circle of professional scholars may, in the long run, derive the greatest benefits from a reintroduction to Jewish legal texts and principles.

For many, if not most, modern Jews, Jewish law has tended to become identified with purely ritual matters, or with problems of marriage regimen or personal status, which often seem so abstruse, convoluted, or antiquated that they repel interest rather than invite it. Jewish law, unfortunately, is often perceived as a phenomenon somehow remote from the course of daily work and the concerns of ordinary people. Even for many Jews who tend to be religiously observant, large portions of the law have lost their applicability and have receded into the deep background of memory. In particular, the Jewish civil and criminal law, as expressed in the Hebrew Bible and as modified and expanded in rabbinic literature, has fallen into desuetude. Of course, the principal reason for this modern view of traditional civil and criminal law is simply that Jews enjoy equality and dignity before the secular law which has clearly preempted the civil and criminal areas. Most Jews of the Diaspora today would undoubtedly feel that the benefits of secular citizenship, including equality before the law, more than make up for the loss of Jewish jurisdiction. And, for such Jews today, the thought of a revival of such Jewish jurisdiction overtaxes the power of imagination. But the rise of a basic perception of Jewish law as somehow a remote and rarefied, if not downright esoteric, branch of study is, at the least, most unfortunate.

Professor Bazak's anthology is carefully selected from just those areas of Jewish law which have, in the past two hundred-odd years, ceased to be observed. This choice of material, excluding as it does the purely ritual law and the marriage law, important as those areas are, subtly affirms a traditional attitude toward the study of the law. Rabbi Ishmael, a second-century jurist, observed that true expertise in Jewish law develops from a painstaking study of the laws dealing with property and finance (*M. Bava Bathra* 10:8). Apart from the fact that the rules in this area of the law are in themselves both legion and difficult, the study of them leads the student willy-nilly to the teeming marketplace where the prescriptions of the law and the requirements of earning a livelihood jostle each other for preeminence in the daily dealings of ordinary people. Traditionally, a student of Talmud began his studies with chapters from the civil and commercial law. Such an introduction no doubt impressed the youngster with the difficulty of the discipline and technique of talmudic debate; but, perhaps without even knowing it, he learned a subtler lesson: Law is intimately engaged with life; the law, if it is to have meaning in society, must function in the heat and press of the marketplace, the shop, the hiring hall, and wherever men strive and strain to earn a livelihood. The Talmud did not greet the novice with a delicate web of abstractions; it rather ushered him into a clamorous world of real people who were not strangers to human foibles and faults. So the student learned early that law and life could not be easily sundered. No matter how far the student went in his studies, and no matter how theoretical those studies became (and advanced talmudic learning is a challenge to the subtlest minds and the most skilled abstract thinkers), the first lessons from the laws of business and commerce were never forgotten. The law, at bottom, meant involvement with the commonplace problems and controversies that characterize human endeavor.

Thus it is that Professor Bazak wisely chose samples of rabbinic jurisprudence that reflect a primary lesson about Jewish legal study. The law flourishes in the midst of human activity; it addresses the problems and quarrels of life directly and forcefully.

Despite the desuetude of much of the traditional law for most modern Jews of the Diaspora, there are signs of renewed interest in Jewish law. The revival of this interest in Jewish law among Jewish laymen is possibly strongest among Jewish youth, particularly college-age youth. These young men and women are often able to discover, test, and enjoy their Jewish heritage in the atmosphere of intellectual stimulation and personal growth found at the university, particularly if the university maintains a Jewish studies program. This revival of interest certainly does not presage a movement to restore civil and criminal jurisdiction to rabbinical courts. It is rather a growing recognition that Jewish legal literature is a uniquely powerful statement of the thrust and direction of Jewish ethics. The talmudic jurists often introduced ethical considerations into their formulations and discussions of the law. It follows, then, that rabbinic jurists, when framing and writing their cases, could not avoid (even if they wished to) developing decisions which say as much about ethical standards as they do about technical jurisprudence. This book reveals in a small measure both the legal and the ethical content of traditional rabbinic decisions on civil and criminal matters. The modern reader may be surprised at the range and scope of the decisions, but such surprise is merely a phase of coming to understand the basic principle that Jewish law is bound up with Jewish life in all its detail. It is but a step from that idea to the conclusion that the ethical content of the law is similarly relevant to life. Hopefully, an acquaintance with the legal literature will assist modern Jews in working out a better-articulated style of Jewish life for themselves.

The presence of Jewish studies departments or courses in many universities fulfills, in part at least, the dream of the nineteenth-century Wissenschaft des Judentums scholars who hoped to see Jewish studies accepted into the program of the modern university. This fulfillment, however, brings with it the obligation to provide the sorts of materials which the modern student can effectively use, particularly if the student has but a limited knowledge of Hebrew. The more of Jewish literature of all types available in translation, the greater the possibilities for stimulating and increasing the present interest in Jewish studies on campus. It should, however, be made clear that a translation does not necessarily reduce the desire to study the original language of the text; it becomes, rather, an intermediate stage along the way toward fuller knowledge, which may include the study of the language of the original. But for those students, and others, who for various reasons cannot undertake the study of the original language, the translation provides a link, a connection, with the original that is, in the long run, worthwhile. So while the rediscovery of the past may assist the layman toward fuller Jewish knowledge and expression, the Jewish student may have an especially rich opportunity and motivation to seek out the Jewish heritage and give it fresh expression in his or her life style.

Indeed, in some communities there is a revived interest in local Jewish conciliation or arbitration panels that could hear disputes between Jews on a variety of matters: landlord-tenant relations, buyer-seller relations, and the like. These panels would in no sense usurp the jurisdiction of the civil or criminal courts; they would, rather, offer an alternative to litigation, a mode of resolving difficulties amicably, before matters pass to the stage of formal proceedings. Moreover, these panels would necessarily measure the validity of claims and arguments against the principles and provisions of Jewish law. The greater the awareness that Jewish law is indeed rich in resources for the settlement of modern disputes, the greater the potentiality of success for these panels.

The revival of interest in Jewish law, whether among scholars or laymen, is a fortunate fact of modern Jewish life. Books and articles on the subject are hopefully more than exercises in esoterica, of more than purely academic moment. Professor Bazak and I offer this translation of responsa in the hope that it may further the revival of interest in Jewish law and reacquaint modern Jewish men and women with a unique and lively treasure of their heritage.

Finally, one might wonder whether this work is "scholarly" or "popular." This is a judgment that depends upon point of view. On the one hand, difficult material has not been deleted; the texts are translated with due respect for both accuracy and clarity (see Translator's Note); and the sources and references are usually "scholarly" ones. In this regard, then, the work is certainly not a primer or a popular introduction to the material. On the other hand, the work is not necessarily for scholars of rabbinic lore. One need not be a talmudic sage to appreciate these cases. Thus the book is certainly not an advanced and abstruse examination of Jewish law of interest to experts only. It attempts to provide a sample, and only a sample, of important rabbinic decisions for those who might relish the chance to get acquainted with some real people and real problems from the Jewish past.

Throughout the process of translation and annotation, Professor Bazak was most helpful and gracious. He made my work a pleasure. Mr. Harvey Horowitz, librarian of the Hebrew Union College-Jewish Institute of Religion in Los Angeles, and his staff accorded me the most expert and sympathetic assistance at all times. The secretarial staff of the HUC-JIR in Los Angeles and my dear wife, Marjorie, worked hard on the typescript. Profoundest thanks are due them all.

Stephen M. Passamaneck
Los Angeles, California
January 1977

# TRANSLATOR'S NOTE

TRANSLATING the literature of a past time and place into the idiom of present time and present place is an adventurous undertaking. The adventure is all the more alluring when the literature is technical, a fact which increases the degree of difficulty inherent in any translation. The responsa translated here represent a sampling of a particularly fascinating genre of rabbinic literature; they are the written opinions and advices handed down by rabbinic jurists on points of Jewish law and practice. Yet they are more than reported cases in the ordinary meaning of the term. They are a record of inestimable value to the historian, the linguist, the anthropologist, the sociologist, the geographer, as well as to the lawyer. The responsa literature often remarks upon features of life or manners or practice in the course of examining intricate legal problems. The remarks may be germane or merely offered en passant; but they preserve a specific view of a past time and place, a past practice or belief, in a fashion that no other Jewish literature does. The translator, therefore, lives constantly in the world of the past and the world of the present while trying to render the idiom of the past into the idiom of the present.

Since Jewish tradition has lovingly preserved the responsa, not as volumes of history or sociology, but as a reservoir of legal opinion, the technical nature of these legal documents prompts some detailing of the problems faced in translating them and a word or two on the solutions which attempted to overcome or minimize the problems. First, there is the problem of language itself. The texts were originally written in the technical jargon of rabbinic jurists; this specialized language is composed of rabbinic Hebrew with an admixture of Aramaic. The idiom is largely drawn from the idiom of the Babylonian Talmud and, occasionally, from the Hebrew Bible. But each authority, in phrasing his opinions, exhibits his own literary skill, whether great or meager. The responsa literature is not a mere recasting of talmudic phrases, or of citations of other rabbinic works, but it has its own grace and style. At times it is lucid, at times ornate, at times lean and direct, and at times convoluted in both thought and phrase. The translator, perforce, picks a path through this language which, it is hoped, will make sense to the modern reader. Moreover, there is the problem of technical terminology. Many of the Hebrew and Aramaic terms are part of the technical legal lexicon of the rabbis. Often these terms *appear* to reflect the same meaning as some term in Anglo-American or Roman law that might be familiar to the modern reader. Yet care must be exercised. The more familiar legal term may have its own subtleties and connotations which could somewhat distort the Hebrew term it translates. Then, too, there is the sort of problem occasioned by the range of meaning of a single Hebrew noun. For instance, the noun *ones*, in various contexts, could be rendered by anything from "forcible rape" to "vis major" to "duress" to "accident." Suffice it to say that great care has been taken with the problem of technical terminology. Au fond, Jewish law and the other great systems of law perceive things in their own special ways; they differ; and sometimes, despite all efforts, some distortion may emerge in a translation. Apologies are herewith tendered for any such flaws that the reader may discover.

There is another problem occasioned by the nature of the material. The authorities who wrote responsa were experts in the Talmud and related literature; and as a rule the addressees of the responsa were also well versed in the law. Often a respondent would cite a talmudic rule or case by giving the first word or two of the relevant passage. The addressee would understand the reference in toto; the few introductory words served to summon up an entire context of argument, counter-argument, and decision in much the same way that a leading case in the common law can be brought rather fully to mind by a simple reference to, for example, *Jones* v. *Smith*. The translator's problem is that the introductory talmudic phrase will not assist the reader who is unfamiliar with the Talmud. Then, too, if the talmudic cases were tucked away in notes, the reader would be constantly darting between text and notes in order to follow the sense of the responsum. In order to assist the reader, the talmudic cases have been paraphrased and inserted into the body of the text. Admittedly, this is a liberty with the actual texts of the responsa; however, the inserted paraphrases do in fact merely make explicit for the modern reader what was implicit for the talmudic expert. Just as the few words of Talmud brought a point fully and clearly to mind for the medieval authorities, the paraphrases, it is hoped, will keep the modern reader informed and aware of the points of law under notice without disturbing the overall sense of the responsum. As a rule the paraphrases are based on Professor Bazak's excellent notes and references in Hebrew. His notes, as it were, have been inserted into the text itself for greater clarity of argument.

Another problem in translation is syntax and grammar. The responsa often have their own elegance and grace; they always have their own style. That style does not always commend itself to ready rendering into English. It is hoped that the renderings adopted here do not overly distort or confuse the reader. Care has been taken to make the English as clear as possible; and often punctuation has been specially employed to make the relationships of various phrases clearer. Some clarifying words or phrases are placed in parentheses.

Just as some material has been inserted for greater clarity, some has been omitted. Occasionally the inquirer inserts some rather complicated terms of address or compliments to the respondent; and the respondent may laud the inquirer in similar fashion. These brief passages combine biblical and rabbinic phrases. They are ornate and often poetic. Unfortunately, their grace and elegance are totally lost in translation. What is delicate and appealing in one language may be florid or turgid in another. Thus they have been omitted. The omissions do not affect the questions and answers themselves.

All amplifications, insertions, and omissions notwithstanding, no attempt has been made to alter the arguments themselves in order to popularize or simplify them. Moreover, certain passages are deliberately couched in a rather formal and antique English so that, it is hoped, an echo of the solemn style of the Hebrew original might be detected.

One other alteration of Professor Bazak's compilation deserves mention. His work arranged the material chronologically by author, so that the earliest authority and his works appeared first. In this translation, the material has been rearranged under general subject headings; the variety in the subject matter made precise headings for general categories impossible. Some materials may easily fit into more than one section, but they could be included under only one rubric. The attempt was made to categorize each responsum under the heading that appeared most closely to suggest the major theme of the text. The Hebrew original also had a biographical sketch as a preface to each section. These biographical notes have been collected and arranged as a separate unit. Professor Bazak agreed to all these modifications in the translation.

Again, the translator herewith apologizes to the reader for any unclarities which may yet lurk in the renderings of the texts.

[This special edition of *Jewish Law and Jewish Life* is being published in fascicle form. Each fascicle contains the entire frontmatter and one of the general subjects. The final edition of this work will contain all the general subjects.]

# INTRODUCTION

THE RESPONSA literature conceals endless treasures of the wisdom, theology, philosophy, history,[1] and folklore[2] of the Jewish people. However, this literature is preeminently a basic and indispensable source for the history of Jewish law. It clarifies how the great Jewish jurists decided their cases in the light of traditional law, cases which emerged in every field of law in the course of everyday life and commerce. While the vast talmudically grounded literature of legal commentary and codification is more abstract and theoretical in approach, the responsa literature brims with life, full of recollections of the give-and-take of the marketplace, of blows struck, of punishments meted out, and much more.

The questions asked include clear and detailed descriptions of life, indeed vignettes of past days, and are often not less significant, on many counts, than the answers.

It is moreover obvious that the answers themselves, which are decisions handed down by rabbinic jurists of unquestioned stature as both legal experts and spiritual mentors, and which are recognized as definitive statements of the law in various areas, represent persuasive legal precedents and are as crucial a factor in a lively and productive Jewish law as the Talmud, the commentaries, and the codes.[3]

Although there is some ground for placing the earliest period of the responsa literature in the late talmudic era,[4] this branch of the legal literature does not clearly emerge until the geonic period, roughly from the seventh to the eleventh centuries in Babylonia. The great geonic academies of Sura and Pumpeditha received queries from all parts of the Diaspora, and those academies issued responsa over the signatures of their geonic rectors. This occurred principally in the early spring month of Adar.[5]

The queries were not restricted to legal subjects. They touched upon

This introduction is partially a paraphrase and partially a translation of Professor Bazak's introduction to the Hebrew edition. I have also translated the notes to his introduction, albeit in a shortened form. S.M.P.

xxi

theology, philosophy, and commentary to difficult talmudic or biblical passages. Rabbi Nathan the Babylonian gives us an eyewitness account of the procedure followed in composing the responsa.

> *Thus was the custom with the responsa: Every day during Adar all the queries which had arrived during the past year were brought to the members of the rabbinical college and leave was granted them to prepare replies. . . . Each man discussed the matters; points were raised and resolved; there was constant give-and-take and the most scrupulous investigations of the questions put. The rector listened to it all. . . . He then stood and reviewed the arguments made until the proper decision became clear. Immediately the scribe was ordered to commit the responsum to writing. This was the daily custom until they had answered all the queries directed to them. . . .At the end of the month all the responsa were read aloud at an assembly of the rabbinical college, and the rector signed them. They were then dispatched to the addressees.*

The responsa were at first written in Aramaic; later they were composed in Hebrew and even in Arabic.[6]

After the geonic period, the major centers for the composition of responsa were Spain (e.g., R. Isaac Alfasi, Joseph ibn Migash, and Maimonides, a Spanish refugee who flourished in Egypt!) and France (e.g., Rashi, R. Jacob Tam, Abraham b. David, and Eliezer b. Nathan).

In the thirteenth century the principal authors of responsa in Spain were Moses b. Nahman, Solomon b. Adret, and Nissim b. Gerondi; in Germany the principal author was Meir of Rothenburg.

In the fourteenth century the leading Spanish masters were Asher b. Yehiel (born in Germany, emigrated to Spain) and Isaac b. Sheshet.

From the fifteenth to the eighteenth centuries, the centers for composition of responsa were Italy, Turkey, Germany, and Poland. During this period, the responsa became longer, the legal essays more complex, and, occasionally, the intricacy of argumentation unfortunately prevailed over clarity of thought and expression. Israel Isserlein and Israel of Bruna, the outstanding authors of responsa from this period, were in Germany; in Italy, Joseph Colon and Judah Minz; in Turkey, Jacob Berab, Levi ibn Habib, Elijah Mizrahi, and Moses Alshkar. The major authors of responsa in sixteenth-century Poland were Moses Isserles, Solomon Luria, and Meir of Lublin; contemporaneously in Turkey the chief authors of responsa were Joseph Karo, Samuel de Medina, and David ibn Zimra.

In the seventeenth century, the great German scholar Jair Haim Bacharach and the great Turkish scholar Joseph di Trani were the most notable authors of responsa. In the eighteenth century, the major figures in responsa literature were Jacob Emden in Germany and Ezekiel Landau in Bohemia. Only the chief authorities have been named; the responsa literature was not limited to their work, of course. Indeed, responsa continue to flourish to the present time, particularly in traditionally observant communities which are faced with the profound changes in modern life due to advances in science and technology.[7]

## Collections of Responsa

The collections of responsa which have come down to us were gathered and arranged by those who received them in order to develop and maintain a body of case law on which to base further decisions. In one of Isaac b. Sheshet's responsa the replies were sometimes delayed.[8] As it was the practice of having students write up the case from the master's notes, the reason for that particular delay was that the students were busy with their own work and none was available for the chore of transcription. The replies were dispatched by messenger, and occasionally the author wrote a brief reply in order not to delay the messenger overlong.[9]

The responsa of one authority may at times have been included in a collection of responsa by another master.[10] This has at times caused misidentification of authorship. Responsa were also found scattered through other legal works (e.g., commentaries) or on the flyleaves of other books. Rabbi Jacob Moellin has left us a description of his discovery of a manuscript responsum in a book of biblical commentary which someone had brought to him for his inspection. At times the responsa of several authors appeared in one collection;[11] some responsa are as yet unpublished, extant only in manuscript form.[12]

Generally only the essence of the query is presented at the beginning of the responsum, and the reply itself may furnish further facts that afford a fuller description of the dispute. However, there are responsa which have simply omitted important details of the query, and it is easy to misread and misunderstand the responsum in such a case. Some responsa collections were supplied with an index—either by the author or one of his students—and these indexes may contain a crucial fact or two not mentioned in the question or the answer.[13]

## The Language of the Responsa

The responsa are a rich mine for the history of the Hebrew language. Many of the authors composed their responsa with a high degree of literary skill reflecting a thorough familiarity with the literary and linguistic resources of Hebrew. The responsa are often prefaced or concluded with poetic allusions and figurative language drawn from biblical or talmudic sources.

The earlier responsa were as a rule rather terse;[14] the later responsa are more detailed. Many responsa have come down to us with the text in rather bad condition because of copyists' errors, publishers' errors, or the unfortunate results of censorship.[15] Occasionally an alteration in a text, originally designed to placate a censor, has rendered a responsum's argumentation obscure and confusing.[16] It is the task of scholarship to examine manuscripts and early printed editions in order to reestablish the correct texts. Such considerations obliged scholars to work on new and scientific editions of the responsa literature based on manuscripts and first editions. Unfortunately, few such editions have appeared.[17]

## Responsa Literature and the Renaissance of Jewish Law

With the establishment of the State of Israel and Jewish national independence, it was logical that the Jewish legal system should similarly experience a renaissance. It would seem appropriate that, instead of dependence on the English common law and other systems of law, Jewish jurists in Israel should turn to the rules and precedents of Jewish law for guidance and direction, since these rules and precedents are, in fact, the result of centuries of dealing with the legal problems of daily life in the context of the sources of Jewish law and the culture, spirit, and life style of the Jewish people. At present it is quite clear that this expectation has not been fulfilled. One of the root causes for this, although legal scholars of all factions voice their regrets about it, is the simple fact that the sources of Jewish law seem to have become a relatively unknown and esoteric branch of study.[18]

The codes and responsa emerged in periods when constant, penetrating, and profound study of talmudic lore was the inherited task of every educated Jewish man. This regular daily study was the obligation of men, young and old, who laid claim to even average intellectual and spiritual gifts.[19]

When the number of fields of study and scientific investigation available to Jews increased and the conditions of Jewish life changed—in the nineteenth and twentieth centuries—the brilliant period of Jewish study faded. Expertise in talmudic lore is no longer the portion of every educated Jew—even if he has some religious training. Moreover, one who has not attended a school which devotes the larger portion of its curriculum to Torah, in its fullest implications, is not really equipped to study talmudic lore on his own. Even those who are religiously trained may not always be able to work with talmudic legal materials without great effort and exertion.

However, Torah was never intended to be purely esoteric wisdom, and one should never blandly accept the fact that, in the modern world, distinguished Jewish jurists, and other intellectuals, are not easily able to turn to the sources of Jewish traditional law or to comprehend them without excessive strain and difficulty. The task is therefore to open the door to this area so that (to paraphrase the Passover Haggadah) "anyone who wishes to enjoy this marvelous intellectual experience may do so." The task will be accomplished if the largest possible group of scholars would concentrate on the preparation and publication of the major works of Jewish legal literature in scientifically edited and properly annotated form.

The responsa literature especially needs this kind of attention in order to render it a proper part of the intellectual heritage available to both jurists and other educated men and women. Only when this familiarity with concepts and sources is achieved will it be possible to include the splendid traditional legal sources, in a full and productive fashion, in the administration of justice in Israel. In view of all of this, I have compiled this present work, *Mishpat Vehalakhah: Mivhar Teshubot,* whose purpose is to present the rabbinical responsa to the educated Jewish reader.[20]

This volume is an anthology of responsa covering the period from the end of the geonic era to the Spanish Expulsion of 1492. The responsa, taken from the works of the most famous principal authors, deal with civil and criminal law. The cases are edited and annotated as fully as possible. References to biblical, talmudic, and post-talmudic sources are supplied (with further annotation where necessary); difficult Hebrew idioms and even relatively simple Aramaic words and idioms, as well as abbreviations, are explained in notes. Additional references to secondary sources relevant to the matter under notice are also supplied in notes. There are also biographical notes and notes on the printed editions from which the responsa are taken.

As far as possible, the first-edition texts are followed in order to avoid the unfortunate results of censorship and poor transcription.

The general rule governing choice of responsa is that each text should have some relevance to a legal question or problem that may still come before a modern court. The attempt has been made to exclude texts which are too long and complex and which would overburden the reader. As in any anthology, the choice of material has been somewhat subjective. I make no claim to have chosen the best, the most important, or the most interesting of the responsa available. Many eminent authors of responsa are not even mentioned in this anthology because their works did not contain enough of the sort of thing I was looking for and simply because the book would have become far too huge if each author were represented.

---

I wish to express my profoundest thanks to my teacher, mentor, and rabbi, Rabbi Solomon Joseph Zevin, who has constantly guided and assisted me ever since my youth and who encouraged me to publish this book.

I wish to acknowledge my obligation to Mr. Haninah Ben-Menahem who read the manuscript with great care, who gave me the benefit of his special knowledge of law, and who double-checked all the sources cited here.

My thanks also go to my good friend Mr. Israel Ta-Shema who was kind enough to read the introductions to the various sections and made many useful suggestions; to the Bibliographical Bureau at the Hebrew University and its director, Mr. Naftali Ben-Menahem, who advised me and put the resources of the bureau at my disposal; to Mr. Zand and his colleagues at the National Library, by whose kind permission the photographs of pages from various first editions of responsa are reproduced here. A special note of thanks is tendered Dr. Moses Spitzer who did an excellent job on the format and design of the book.

The Research Fund of the Bar-Ilan University partially supported the publication of this book, and I take this opportunity to extend my thanks for that assistance.

# Notes

1. See A. Marx, "Aims of Jewish Historiography," *Publications of the Jewish Historical Society* (New York, 1918), pp. 11-32, and see also Israel Abrahams, *Jewish Life in the Middle Ages.*

2. Isaac Kahana, "Ba'ayot Folkloriot Besifrut Hateshuvot," *Jubilee Volume in Honor of Dr. Simon Federbush* (Jerusalem: Mosad Harav Kook, 1961), pp. 227-33.

3. See especially Joseph ibn Migash's case, No. 114; other authorities express the same view, e.g., Jacob Moellin, No. 72; see also Kahana in the *Bar-Ilan Yearbook* (memorial volume for Prof. P. Horgin, pp. 270-81).

4. *B. Temurah* 12b, *B. Hullin* 95b, *B. Bava Bathra* 41b, and others.

5. See also Assaf, "Hakatvu Hageonim et Teshuvotehem Rak Bekalah Deadar?" in *Yediot Hamachon Lemada' Hayahadut*, Book 1, pp. 49-54.

6. See Assaf, *Tekufat Hageonim Vesifruta* (Jerusalem: Mosad Harav Kook, 1955).

7. See Boaz Cohen, *Kuntres Hateshubot* (Budapest, 1930, and Jerusalem, 1970).

8. See Isaac b. Sheshet's case, No. 261.

9. See Isaac b. Sheshet's case, No. 261; the introductory remarks in a responsum often permit a rather accurate dating of the text, at least in respect to the month and day, if not the year.

10. For instance, a responsum by Eliezer b. Nathan (Case No. 98) has been attributed to Meir of Rothenburg; cf. *Kizoth Hahoshen* to *Shulhan Arukh, Hoshen Mishpat* 322:1.

11. Case No. 74.

12. The work of Rabbi Joseph Kepah is particularly noteworthy here; he has published a number of collections of responsa which were extant only in manuscript before, e.g., the responsa of Yom Tov b. Abraham Ashbili, published in 1959.

13. Moses Minz's index to his own responsa furnishes significant detail on occasion.

14. Maimonides is often exceedingly brief.

15. See Ibn Migash's case, No. 114.

16. See Isaac b. Sheshet's case, No. 236. The phrase "capital punishment" was changed to "punishment" because of censorship.

17. The work of the Meikize Nirdamin, first in Europe and presently in Israel, and the work of the Mosad Harav Kook are particularly praiseworthy in the matter of developing and publishing modern scientific editions of rabbinic legal texts.

18. See Bazak, *Hamishpat Haivri Umedinat Yisrael* (Jerusalem: Mosad Harav Kook, 1969).

19. Rabbi Joshua Falk, sixteenth century, scolds laymen who devoted their paltry (!) three or four hours of daily study to Talmud alone, without any study of the codes; see the *Sifthe Cohen* commentary to *Shulhan Arukh, Yoreh Deah* 246, n. 5.

20. Dr. Solomon B. Freehof has made some progress in this task; see his *The Responsa Literature* (Philadelphia: Jewish Publication Society, 1955) and *A Treasury of Responsa* (Philadelphia: Jewish Publication Society, 1963).

# BIOGRAPHICAL NOTES

THESE BIOGRAPHICAL notes merely give some basic historical background for each of the eminent rabbis whose responsa are translated in this book. They do not pretend to do anything more. At the end of some of these sketches there are references to various sources which provide fuller data.

The *Encyclopaedia Judaica* and the *Jewish Encyclopedia* both contain articles on the respondents represented in this book. Major works on Jewish history and literature also furnish more complete information on them. Solomon Freehof's *The Responsa Literature* (Philadelphia: Jewish Publication Society, 1955) and *A Treasury of Responsa* (Philadelphia: Jewish Publication Society, 1963) are excellent additional sources on the jurists and their work. Occasionally the work of a particular authority is used as the major source for a detailed study of that authority's historical period. Such studies are duly noted in the brief sketches. Most of the secondary literature on the authors of responsa is in Hebrew; but there is a sufficient amount of secondary material in English in the various encyclopedia articles so that the reader can gain a reasonable familiarity with the general nature of the literature and some of its chief representatives.

*R. Joseph ibn Migash, 1077-1141,* Seville and Lucena. Ibn Migash was an outstanding pupil of the eleventh-century respondent and codifier Isaac of Fez (acronym: Alfasi) who designated him as his successor in the presidency of the rabbinical college at Lucena. Ibn Migash served in that position for thirty-eight years, until his own death. Even so great a figure as Maimonides, in the introduction to his commentary on the Mishnah, praised Ibn Migash's wisdom and acuteness.

Ibn Migash composed, in addition to responsa, novellae to several tractates of the Talmud. His responsa were originally in Arabic; about two hundred of them have been translated into Hebrew. These responsa were first printed in Salonika, 1791; an annotated edition of Ibn Migash's responsa, prepared by Rabbi Wolf Leiter, of blessed memory, of Pittsburgh, was published in New York, 1954.

*R. Eliezer b. Nathan, ca. 1090-1170.* One of the outstanding figures among the Franco-German authors of talmudic novellae, the Tosafists, Eliezer was a liturgical poet as well as a legal authority. He was a younger contemporary of Isaac b. Asher Halevi, the famous Riba. Eliezer lived for a while in France and in Bohemia. He had knowledge of the customs of Jewish communities as far afield as Greece and Russia. Among his descendants was Eliezer b. Joel Halevi.

Eliezer's principal work was the *Eben Haezer,* the word *Eben* being a Hebrew acronym for his name. This work, a collection of decisions and interpretations in the field of Jewish law and custom, is the earliest extant work describing the culture of German Jewry.

Eliezer also wrote various types of liturgical poetry, some of which are included in the Ashkenazic rites for holy days. In addition, he wrote a book of remembrances commemorating the tragedies suffered by the Rhenish Jewish communities in 1096. This has been reprinted in *Sefer Gezeroth Ashkenaz Vetzorfat,* ed. A. M. Habermann (Jerusalem, 1946).

Eliezer is mentioned often in Irving Agus's *The Heroic Age of Franco-German Jewry.*

*R. Moses b. Maimon (acronym: Rambam), Maimonides, 1135-1204,* Spain and North Africa. Rambam deserves mention among the greatest jurists and legal minds of all nations, even though he is primarily known today as a philosopher. Due to the anti-Jewish activity following the Almohade conquest of his native Cordova, Rambam, then thirteen, fled with his family, eventually settling in Egypt. He died there in 1204, and his body was taken to Tiberias for burial.

Maimonides's three principal works are his *Commentary on the Mishnah,* his philosophical work, *Guide to the Perplexed,* and his massive *Mishneh Torah,* a restatement and rearrangement of the totality of Jewish law up to his time. His other works include his responsa, originally written in Arabic, talmudic commentary, and treatises on medicine. Maimonides was a practicing physician of renown in addition to being the foremost rabbinic jurist of his time.

*R. Meir b. Todros Halevi Abulafia, 1170-1244,* Burgos and Toledo. Meir settled in Toledo when his father received a rabbinic appointment in that city. In time Meir also became a judge in the rabbinical court of Toledo. He was one of the chief rabbinic figures in Castile and had the respect of another great figure of the place and period, R. Moses b. Nahman (Nahmanides).

R. Meir's principal work was a collection of novellae to the entire Babylonian Talmud. He compiled this while he was still a young man. Only two tractates of this work are extant, *Bava Bathra* and *Sanhedrin*. The work is a minute examination of every subject raised in the Talmud and is justly distinguished for its acuity.

Another of his major works, published in Florence, 1750, dealt with the peculiarities of the text of the Five Books of Moses.

See Baer, *History of the Jews in Christian Spain* (Philadelphia: Jewish Publication Society, 1961), and A. Neuman, *The Jews in Spain* (Philadelphia: Jewish Publication Society, 1942).

*R. Meir b. Baruch of Rothenburg, 1215-1293.* This R. Meir was the greatest of the German rabbinic legal authorities, and he is often described as the "father" of modern Ashkenazic tradition.

R. Meir was born in Worms and studied under Isaac b. Moses of Vienna, the compiler of the legal work *Or Zarua*. He also studied in the rabbinic academies of France, where he collected responsa, novellae, decisions, and traditions, all of which he took back to his academy in Germany. While R. Meir was in France, he witnessed the public burning of talmudic literature in Paris in 1242. He composed a dirge to commemorate that tragedy.

R. Meir spent most of his life in Rothenburg, where he founded a great rabbinic academy which became the most important one in Germany. His students became the great teachers of their generation and the great judges of the German communities. The most outstanding among R. Meir's pupils were Rabbenu Asher b. Yehiel, R. Mordecai b. Hillel, and R. Haim b. Isaac "Or Zarua."

Both individuals and communities in all parts of Central Europe looked upon R. Meir as the most authoritative scholar and judge of Jewish law; and they addressed a huge volume of questions to him, questions which involved matters of law regarding both individuals and communities.

With the rise of anti-Jewish persecution in Germany, R. Meir resolved to go to Palestine and was actually en route there when he was recognized by an apostate Jew, turned in to the government as a fugitive, and put into the custody of Emperor Rudolph I at the castle of Ensisheim, Alsace, June 25, 1286. The emperor set an inordinately high price on R. Meir. Rabbenu Asher, R. Meir's pupil, soon began to collect the necessary sum, but R. Meir himself forbade the communities to ransom him—first, in order that other potentates not adopt a similar technique of extortion to wring more and more money from the Jews and, second, to fulfill the talmudic precept (*B. Gittin* 45a) that, as a matter of public policy and welfare, communities were not to give in to extortion in the matter of redeeming captives.

R. Meir remained incarcerated at Ensisheim until his death, on April 27, 1293. Fourteen years later, on April 19, his body was given to the Jewish community for burial.

During his incarceration R. Meir remained an active correspondent and author of responsa.

Apart from responsa, decisions, and customs, he wrote novellae to several tractates of the Talmud. E. E. Urbach notes that the Tosafot to tractate *Yoma,* customarily published with the talmudic text, were edited and arranged by R. Meir. Leopold Zunz has listed nineteen liturgical poems from R. Meir's hand, of which some are included in the Ashkenazic rites for the Day of Atonement and the Ninth of Av. In 1938 a book of R. Meir of Rothenburg's customs, responsa, decisions, and prayer services for the entire cycle of the year was published. Professor Irving Agus translated R. Meir's responsa into English: *R. Meir of Rothenburg,* 2 vols. (Philadelphia, 1947).

The decisions of R. Meir are incorporated and discussed by the score in the rabbinic legal literature of the fourteenth and fifteenth centuries and to a degree in the rabbinic legal literature of the sixteenth century.

*R. Solomon b. Abraham Adret (Rashba).* Born in Barcelona in 1235, Rashba became the most distinguished son of an eminent family. He was the pupil of both Moses b. Nahman, the illustrious Nahmanides, and the equally illustrious Jonah Gerondi. During his earlier years, Rashba conducted a banking business and numbered the king of Aragon among his debtors. However, his career as a banker never interfered with his fifty-year tenure as the rabbi of his native Barcelona. He eventually gave up banking to devote himself to study and communal administration and soon became generally recognized as an expert in talmudic law and a legal authority of the first rank.

Rashba probably wrote about ten thousand responsa (somewhat over three thousand are extant). His opinions are cited as authoritative on innumerable pages of rabbinic legal literature. These responsa were written with clarity and excellent logic and touch upon all areas of Jewish law and thought.

Rashba possessed not only intellectual strength and courage but humility and a desire for communal harmony as well. He recognized philosophy as an intellectual discipline of merit at a time when the

Spanish Jewish community was bitterly divided over the question of "religious" versus "secular" learning. He was also familiar with Spanish secular legal systems. In his old age, Rashba attempted to achieve a compromise solution for the problem of "secular" learning by issuing a ban against the study of philosophy by students under twenty years of age; this ban was to be in effect for only fifty years.

Among his principal pupils were Bahya b. Asher and Yom Tov b. Ashbili.

Rashba died in 1310, at the age of seventy-five. See Isidore Epstein, *The Responsa of Rabbi Solomon b. Adret* (London, 1925; reprint ed., New York, 1968).

*R. Haim Eliezer b. R. Isaac "Or Zarua."* R. Haim's father, R. Isaac of Vienna, compiler of the compendium of law named *Or Zarua*, died while R. Haim was still a child. The son learned of his famous father from relatives who raised him. R. Haim lived in the second half of the thirteenth century, and he studied under R. Meir of Rothenburg. He was a school fellow of Rabbenu Asher and R. Mordecai b. Hillel. He served as rabbi at Weiner-Neustadt (Austria), at Cologne for a while, at Prague, and then at Mainz. In 1301 R. Haim wrote the *Small Or Zarua*, an abbreviated version of his father's famous work.

*Rabbenu Asher b. Yehiel (Rosh).* Rabbenu Asher b. Yehiel was one of the foremost early legal authorities and expositors of the Talmud. He was born in 1250 in Cologne, of a distinguished family; and, after tutelage at home, he went on to become the most famous of Meir of Rothenburg's disciples. R. Meir himself appointed R. Asher to the rabbinic court at Worms; after R. Meir's arrest, R. Asher became the leader of Franco-German Jewry.

Apprehensive that he might be marked for the same fate his teacher had suffered, R. Asher left Germany for Spain in 1304. In Barcelona, in 1304, R. Asher, whose reputation was already established among Ashkenazic Jews, was welcomed cordially and fraternally by the aged Solomon b. Adret, premier rabbi and leader of the Sephardic Jewish world. In 1305 R. Asher moved to Toledo, principal city of Castile, where he had been asked to serve as chief judge and rector of the rabbinical college.

The prime indication of R. Asher's greatness is the acceptance he received in the Spanish Jewish communities which differed vastly from the Franco-German communities in religio-cultural forms and styles. R. Asher's rapid rise to an eminence among the Spaniards, equal to the eminence he had attained among the Germans, distinguishes him as a pivotal figure in the history of Jewish law. As an individual he combined immense expertise in both the Ashkenazic and Sephardic schools of Jewish law and legal methodology to a measure which had never been achieved before his time and perhaps never has been achieved again. R. Asher was the most illustrious of all Spanish rabbis from the death of Rashba in 1310 to the Expulsion in 1492.

When R. Asher came to Spain, he was thunderstruck to discover that Jewish courts, under royal patents, exercised capital jurisdiction. R. Asher quickly added his confirmation to this authority and even seconded a sentence of amputation of the tongue for a defendant found guilty of blasphemy; such punishment was, of course, the usual fate of blasphemers under non-Jewish law at that time in Spain. He also added his authority to the imposition of capital punishment for those found guilty of traitorous acts against the Jewish community.

R. Asher died in Toledo on October 31, 1327. After his death, the leaders of the Toledo community, in an attempt to establish rules for authoritative citations in their communal courts, proposed that the authoritative statement of the law is the one given by Maimonides, except in instances where R. Asher differs with him!

R. Asher's principal work was the *Piske Harosh,* known also as the *Hilkhot Harosh* and the *Asheri.* This work is a series of restatements of the rules and legal argumentation of the Babylonian Talmud with the interpolation of the opinions of rabbinic authorities who wrote prior to Rosh. Rosh also prepared commentaries to the Bible and the Mishnah and novellae to the Talmud.

Rosh's extant responsa number approximately one thousand, and they deal with all areas of rabbinic law. The responsa are arranged according to 108 subjects. In the responsa, R. Asher emerges as a man of broad worldly experience and as a writer with a smooth, clear style. He rendered decisions with a full and incisive mastery of Talmud and talmudic commentary, which to his mind were the *sole authoritative* sources of the law—with which there could be no compromise.

*R. Judah b. Asher (b. Yehiel).* R. Judah was the fourth son of R. Asher b. Yehiel. He was born in Cologne in 1270 and studied at the rabbinical college there, which was headed by his father. While still young he traveled and studied in France and finally settled in Toledo, Spain, where his father later eventually settled. In R. Asher's old age, R. Judah was appointed his father's chief assistant (1321), and after his father's death in 1327 he assumed his father's offices as chief judge and rector of the rabbinic college at Toledo; he was also confirmed by the king of Castile as the chief rabbi of Castile.

R. Judah's court exercised capital jurisdiction on the basis of the authority delegated to the rabbinical court by the government. However, R. Judah admonished the judges to use great restraint and care in the exercise of this authority.

He answered many legal inquiries sent to him from all parts of Spain. He died in 1349, a victim of the Black Death epidemic.

*R. Yom Tov b. Abraham Ashbili (Ritba).* Ritba was born in Seville about the year 1250. He studied in Barcelona under Aaron Halevi and Rashba. He became a judge in Saragossa, and even the secular government recognized his authority and skill in Jewish law. In at least one instance the secular government asked him to review the decision of another rabbinic judge who had sentenced a man to amputation of tongue and hand and to exile from his city. On another occasion, Ritba fearlessly handed down a decision against some rich Jewish families that had abused their rights in some taxation matters. He was seriously wounded when these families avenged themselves on him. Ritba was yet another in the splendid group of jurists and spiritual leaders in thirteenth- and fourteenth-century Spain. He died about 1330.

*R. Nissim b. Reuben Gerondi (Ran).* One of the greatest of the Spanish authorities, Ran served as rabbi, judge, and rector of the rabbinical college in Barcelona in the fourteenth century. He was also a renowned physician. Both Jewish and non-Jewish authorities held him in the highest esteem. His famous pupil, Isaac b. Sheshet, wrote that Ran was incomparably the greatest authority of his age. His fame was such that he dealt with legal inquiries not only from Spain but from France, Italy, and North Africa as well. He died about 1380.

Of his many responsa, only a few score are extant; a collection of his responsa appeared in print for the first time in Rome in 1545. Ran is best known for his commentaries to fourteen tractates of Alfasi's *Epitome*; his commentaries reveal an excellent independent and critical approach.

Abraham Hershman wrote an excellent study on the life of Ran's most famous pupil, *Rabbi Isaac b. Sheshet Perfet and His Times* (New York: Jewish Theological Seminary, 1943), and this book, of course, makes reference to Ran.

*R. Isaac b. Sheshet Perfet (Ribash).* The son of a well-known Barcelona family, Ribash was born in 1326. His teachers were Hasdai Crescas and Ran. In 1372-73 he was forced to leave his native city and went to Saragossa, in Aragon, where he served as rabbi from 1385 until he was forced to flee the persecutions of 1391. Then, 65 years old, Ribash fled to Algiers where he served as chief rabbi and judge. The early period of his tenure as chief rabbi was not without opposition, but he was finally recognized by all factions of the Jewry of Algiers. In order to strengthen his position, he enlisted the support of Saul Astruc, physician royal and lay head of the Algerian Jewish community, and secured royal appointment as the rabbi of the community of Spanish emigres in Algiers. Even Ribash's antagonist, the famous Rabbi Simon Duran, eventually hailed Ribash as a worthy and most excellent choice for the chief rabbinate (Duran's *Responsa*, sec. 1, no. 160).

Ribash died in Algiers in 1408. Hershman's *Rabbi Isaac b. Sheshet Perfet and His Times* is the best study in English on this authority.

*R. Jacob b. Moses Halevi Moellin (Maharil).* R. Jacob Moellin was born in Mainz in 1360 and was one of the greatest of the German rabbis. His father, the chief rabbi of Mainz, was his first teacher. While yet young, Jacob left his native Mainz and went to Wiener-Neustadt to study with R. Shalom b. Isaac from whom he received rabbinical certification. When Moellin's father died in 1387, he was called back to Mainz to fill his father's post. Moellin served as rabbi of Mainz and founded a rabbinical college which became one of the finest and most popular of the time. R. Jacob Weil, of whom more later, attended Moellin's college and has told how Moellin supported his pupils financially (Weil's *Responsa*, no. 133).

Moellin carefully cataloged the customs and rituals of German Jewry, and this work was later published (Sabionetta, 1555), with Moellin's sermons, by Moellin's pupil Elazar b. Jacob. This collection of custom and ritual peculiar to German Jewry became in time the basis for a significant part of Moses Isserles's glosses to the *Shulhan Arukh*, which made that work useful and relevant for Ashkenazic Jewry.

Moellin was also a cantor of some artistic excellence. His melody for *Kol Nidre* is still part of the expert cantor's repertoire.

Toward the end of his life, Moellin moved to Worms, where he died on September 13, 1427. He was buried close to the grave of Meir of Rothenburg.

The best secondary references in English are Sidney Steinman's *Custom and Survival* (New York: Bloch Publishing Co., 1963) and

Solomon Eidelberg's *Jewish Life in Austria in the XV Century* (Philadelphia, 1962).

*R. Simon b. Zemah Duran (Rashbatz).* Rabbi Duran was born on the island of Majorca in 1361. His father was learned in both religious and secular fields. The Duran family had come to Majorca in 1305 from southern France because of anti-Jewish persecution. Other members of this large and distinguished family came to Majorca in 1391 because of persecution in Spain.

Duran studied both religious and secular subjects. He had a knowledge of philosophy, logic, astronomy (astrology), and languages; while he did not pursue mathematics or astronomy to any great degree, he was able to draw up astronomical tables and to calculate accurately the movements of the moon and various stars.

Rashbatz made a living as a physician and surgeon, which were honored and well-paid professions on Majorca.

In 1391 the pressure of persecution drove him and his family to abandon their property and flee to Algiers. In Algiers he was not able to support himself as a physician owing to popular reliance on folk medicine and various quack healers. Thus, despite personal reservations, he was compelled to take a paid position as a rabbi.

After Isaac b. Sheshet became chief rabbi and judge by royal appointment, with power to act as sole judge, Duran wrote a responsum excoriating the appointment on both logical and legal grounds, although he did recognize and revere Ribash as a great sage. The controversy ended when the king decided that other rabbis could also act as judges upon receiving licensure from Ribash. Since the quarrel had an ending acceptable to Duran, he did not publish the bitter denunciation of Ribash.

Duran was the youngest of the three illustrious rabbis of Algiers, the others being Ribash and Isaac Bonastruc. Nevertheless, the elder rabbis permitted Duran to promulgate a number of ordinances dealing with marriage law and then gave their approval to them.

After Ribash's death in 1408, Duran became chief rabbi of Algiers. He wrote many responsa to queries addressed to him from North Africa and elsewhere. Even Ribash himself asked his opinion on legal matters. Duran's responsa are generally lengthy but formulated with clarity and logic. In the three-volume edition of Duran's responsa (Amsterdam, 1738-41) there are more than nine hundred cases which are valuable both as legal documents and historical records. His works exhibit a surgical precision of logical arguments which move inexorably to inescapable conclusions. Duran died in 1444.

The best work in English on Duran is Isidore Epstein's *The Responsa of Rabbi Simon b. Zemach Duran as a Source of History of the Jews of North Africa* (London, 1930; reprint ed., New York: Hermon Press, 1968).

*R. Solomon b. Simon Duran (Rashbash).* Rabbi Solomon b. Simon Duran was the famous son of a famous father, Simon b. Zemah Duran. He was born in Algiers about 1400. He studied with his father and was a brilliant student of Jewish law, not to mention grammar, medicine, and philosophy. While still young, he was appointed an associate to his father's rabbinical court. As Simon grew older, Solomon took over more and more of his father's duties, including the answering of legal questions. When his father died, Solomon succeeded him as chief rabbi of Algiers. In addition to his legal work, he taught and engaged in religious polemics and wrote over six hundred responsa. He died in 1467.

*R. Israel b. Petahiah Isserlein.* R. Israel Isserlein (known also as Israel of Marburg and Israel of Neustadt, two cities where he lived for some time) was the greatest German rabbi of the fifteenth century. He was born in Regensburg in 1390. His best-known work is the collection of responsa *Terumath Hadeshen.* Israel's father died when he was a child, and an uncle took charge of the boy's education. In 1421 Isserlein's uncle and mother were both murdered in anti-Jewish rioting in Vienna. Isserlein fled to Italy. In 1445 he was called back to Austria to assume the rabbinate of Wiener-Neustadt. He headed a rabbinical college there, and many students were attracted to his school. In old age he appointed his son to take over the direction of his school. He died in 1460.

Isserlein maintained a most pious personal regimen. Some of his personal practices were recounted by his student Joseph b. Moses in the introduction to his own work *Leket Yosher* (Berlin, 1903). His other work, *Beure Mahri,* preserves Isserlein's notes and comments to Rashi's talmudic commentary.

As noted above, Isserlein's principal work is the *Terumath Hadeshen* of 354 responsa (the numerical equivalent of *deshen* in Hebrew). A second section, *Pesakim Uketavim* ("Decisions and Notes"), containing 267 responsa collected by his students, was appended to the larger work.

*R. Jacob Weil.* Rabbi Weil was another great German rabbi of the fifteenth century. He studied under Moellin (and apparently under Isserlein) and served as rabbi in Nuremberg, Augsburg, and Erfurt respectively. He was considered a judge whose decisions had great and even definitive merit. Even the great Isserlein and Israel of Brunn sought his opinion on matters of law. Weil is noted for his decision which permitted more than one rabbi to settle and judge cases in a single Ashkenazic community, even if a rabbi who was there first suffered some economic disadvantage because of the newcomer (responsum no. 151).

Eidelberg's *Jewish Life in Austria in the XV Century* supplies background information on Weil.

*R. Israel b. Haim of Brunn.* Israel of Brunn is yet another representative of the superior rabbinate of fifteenth-century Germany and Austria. He was born about 1400 and trained under Weil (who was also his father-in-law) and Isserlein. He began his rabbinate in Brunn but moved to Regensburg because of a dispute with a rabbi who wanted to establish a rabbinical college in Brunn. Israel set up his college in Regensburg and served there for close to thirty years.

In Regensburg, too, Israel of Brunn suffered greatly from quarreling, which developed over the matter of his right to open a rabbinical college in that place and to render legal decisions on marital matters. R. Anshel, the senior rabbi of Regensburg, who had performed all rabbinic functions before Israel arrived, complained bitterly that Israel of Brunn had invaded his territory. Although both Isserlein and Weil rendered decisions which upheld Israel's right to found the college and perform rabbinical functions in Regensburg, the quarreling and backbiting did not stop until Anshel died in 1454.

Israel of Brunn was held hostage by Emperor Frederick III, who sought thereby to speed up collection of a "crown tax" from the Jews of Regensburg. The emperor wanted Israel to excommunicate any Jew of Regensburg who did not surrender a third of his property for this tax. He was freed upon the posting of a substantial surety.

When he was seventy-six Israel was put in prison again, this time because an apostate accused him of the classic slander against Jews: the murder of a Christian child. He was freed when the apostate himself was sentenced to the stake. The date of Israel of Brunn's death is not precisely known.

*R. Moses b. Isaac Minz Halevi (Segel).* This important fifteenth-century German rabbi was born in Mainz. He was a brilliant student and studied under Jacob Weil in Erfurt. While still a young man he accepted the office of rabbi in Wurzburg. He was regularly in contact with Israel of Brunn, Jacob Minz, and Joseph Colon.

When the Jews were expelled from Wurzburg in 1453, Minz returned to his native city, where he became active in the rabbinate and in communal work. He was forced to leave Mainz in the expulsion of 1462. During this tragedy he suffered the loss of his personal property, particularly his library, which included responsa he had written and responsa he had received from his contemporaries. Nevertheless, he continued to write responsa; he was a man of profound and encyclopedic Jewish legal knowledge. In 1469 he accepted the rabbinate of Bamberg. Later he became rabbi in Posen in Poland. He entertained a wish to emigrate to Palestine but never succeeded in making the journey.

Minz edited his responsa himself, furnishing them with an introduction and an occasionally incorrect or misleading index.

*R. Joseph Colon (Maharik).* Joseph Colon was one of the greatest Italian rabbis. As a youngster he lived in Chambery, in the Savoy district. He was possibly a student of Jacob Moellin. Forced to leave Chambery, he became the rabbi of several cities in Northern Italy (Bologna, then Mantua, and finally Pavia). Colon clearly saw that Jewish learning in Italy had to be revived and improved. He took it upon himself to start an elementary school for the training of Jewish children. Later he opened a rabbinical college in Mantua, which attracted more advanced scholars from many distant parts.

Colon generally framed his responsa with the talmudic material as the basis of his decision. He was personally inclined to be strict, but he well realized that the lay community far preferred a lenient judge in religious matters. Nevertheless, he did not shrink from forthright opposition to customs and usages that had no real foundation in the law. Along with his great personal modesty and piety, he was resolute in insisting on the truth and did not hesitate to issue a sharp rebuke to even so great a scholar as Israel of Brunn who had excommunicated a man even though the man had expressed deep remorse for his misdeed and was ready to accept punishment.

Colon died in Pavia in 1480.

See H. Rabinowicz, "Life and Times of Rabbi Joseph Colon" (thesis, University of London, 1947) and the same author's articles in the *Journal of Jewish Studies,* vol. 6 (1955), pp. 166-70, and the *Jewish Quarterly Review,* vol. 47 (1956-57), pp. 336-44.

# BOOK 2

---

## Partnership
### commercial practice
### employer-employee relations
### liability of an expert
### the construction of a contract

---

THIS SECTION consists of thirteen responsa, most of them dealing with various problems of partnership under Jewish law. The partnership is, for many commercial purposes, clearly superior to an enterprise conducted by one person because capital can be pooled, risks can be jointly shared, and business can be transacted with more people and with greater efficiency.

The partnership was not, however, without its pitfalls. The first case deals with the assets of a dissolved partnership. One man is suing his former partners because, quite by mistake, he had accepted a bad account as his share in the distribution of the assets of the old firm. Another case quickly reviews the matter of a man who acted as his partners' agent in the formation of a larger partnership. There is a case on the nature of lawful partnership: a partnership can only be formed for the transaction of lawful business. Other cases review the matters of joint liability in a partnership and the sharing of profits and losses. One case, involving bitter quarrels among partners, is not decided because as presented it did not provide an adequate statement of the facts; yet even without a decision this text discloses a brief sample of a situation which has a surprisingly modern ring to it.

Several cases discuss the significance of commercial practice, the law merchant as it were, for the Jewish court. The usages of businessmen had great and even decisive weight in many cases. One matter reflects the difficulties of businessmen in repaying loans, etc., when the names and values of legal tender changed. Even without the problems of clipped or counterfeit coinage, medieval merchants faced the delicate problem of changes or reissues of the monetary unit.

There are two cases of employer-employee relations which discuss

1

the legality of the dismissal of an employee and the special nature of a contract for teaching Jewish religious subjects.

One case deals with the liability of the professional, or expert, who gives a professional opinion or evaluation. The case has a bearing on various commercial situations involving expert opinion, but the responsibilities and liabilities of the learned professions constitute another and more specialized aspect of this question. Physicians' liabilities are not part of the case presented here.

The last case concerns the construction of a contract which is somewhat unclear because of a grammatical anomaly in the Hebrew document. This particular case might come under a consideration of real property, but it is ultimately a matter of contract and commercial practice. The argument, with its references to masculine and feminine grammatical structures, is actually less complex than it appears to be at first.

S.M.P.

# R. Eliezer b. Nathan

No. 99    Dissolution of a partnership: conditions implied in consent

*Decision:* The plaintiff may sue his former partners for a redistribution of the assets of the former partnership. Owing to the fact that the plaintiff had made a loan on a pledge, which pledge later was used as further security for another loan to the same party, which latter loan was made by the partnership, when the pledgor refused to honor the second debt, plaintiff sought redistribution of the assets since the asset, i.e., the pledge, was, in effect, a bad debt: the pledge was a liability, not an asset. The original distribution was predicated on the belief that the pledge did represent an asset.

*Question:* Reuben loaned silver money to a bishop on the security of a (valuable) pledge. After a while the bishop attended the royal court and some Jews went with him to attend the fair at the court. Reuben formed a partnership there with Simon and Levi, and the three of them went to court to engage in profitable moneylending with their silver. (One asset of the partnership was the security which the bishop had pledged.) The bishop needed more money and asked the three partners for a loan. Reuben said: "You owe me (only) a *zakuk* (i.e., the silver money loaned) on the pledge (which was worth more than the first loan); the partnership will loan you what you wish (on the same pledge)." They made the loan. After a while the partnership dissolved. They divided the assets of the partnership and established Reuben's share as what was owed on that very pledge. Reuben was satisfied and accepted this division of assets. After a while the bishop came to redeem the pledge. The bishop acknowledged the original loan of one *zakuk*, which had been made on the pledge, but denied owing anything else. Reuben went to his former partners and sought a new division of assets. They responded that the partnership was dissolved and they had nothing to do with the pledge, which had originally secured Reuben's

3

loan—made outside the partnership (i.e., before there had been a partnership).

Now, may our teacher instruct us: With whom is the law? Do we say that since the partnership is dissolved the former partners no longer have any involvement in the matter, and Reuben's "field is flooded" (the matter is Reuben's bad luck!), or perhaps the division *is* null and they should redivide assets?

*Answer:* This is my answer—not that I am worthy that you inquire of me—but my opinion inclines toward the view that the division of assets is null and void, whether one takes the opinion of Rav or the opinion of Samuel set forth in the Talmud, *B. Bava Qamma* 9a. There, the matter concerns brothers as heirs, who are considered as partners in respect to the estate. A creditor of the deceased father comes to demand payment. When the heirs divided the estate, they did not set aside an amount to satisfy the creditor, of whose existence the heirs had knowledge. One may say that they arranged the partition of the estate with each fully aware of the risk that the one approached by the creditor would have to bear the loss of satisfying the debt, and the other one would not lose anything. (Both took the risk.) Even in this case Rav said that the partition is null and the loss falls upon both of them. Here, in the pledge case, at the time of the division of the assets, the partners did not contemplate, and certainly did not know of, the eventuality that the bishop would deny his debt. They had no doubts—but were positive that the bishop would pay. How much the more does it follow that Reuben should not absorb the whole loss!

This is true even according to Samuel, who said that the heir has, by reason of the partition of the estate, relinquished any rights to have it redistributed if the creditor comes and collects from him, because both bore the risk and the doubt in respect to which one would be approached for payment. Since Samuel deems the heirs to be, after the partition, like purchasers who should have protected themselves by placing appropriate conditions (on the sale—or partition in this case) and did not do so: they are like purchasers without a warranty. Each one relies upon his own good luck and says, "He won't come to me!" Since this was their state of mind when they partitioned the estate, the heir has relinquished any further remedy and the one who satisfied the debt bears the loss.

Here the partners entertained no doubts because they were of the opinion that the bishop's loan was unquestionably part of their assets, and Reuben, who accepted that account as part of the partnership's assets, was certain that it was a good debt and renounced any rights in assets taken by his fellows. But this renunciation was done under a mistake of fact—and it is not valid! This is like the incident concerning R. Anan in *B. Bava Bathra* 41a.[1] R. Anan had to remove a wall which he had built on land which he erroneously thought was his; his claim of ownership, on the basis of the former owner's assistance in the construction of the wall, was disallowed. The assistance and the construction were wholly due to mistake on the part of the owner. Even an agreement which is validated by a formal acquisition may be held null and void if the formal act was done under a mistake of fact. This is what we find in *B. Gittin* 14a in respect to one of several gardeners who settled their account books among themselves. It was found that one had a small sum left over. The others, in the landlord's presence, told him to give the money to the landlord. This was confirmed by a formal act of acquisition. The gardener later found that *no money* had been left over. The eventual decision was that the formal act of acquisition, when performed because of a mistake of fact, is null and void.

Thus, in this case Reuben was under the impression that the loan was good, and he relied on that impression. He renounced rights to other property of the partnership and caused his fellows to acquire the other property. Now that the loan has proved to be a bad debt, the formal acquisition is null and void.

As for the matter that one partner took money from the division of assets and another took an account receivable, the following argument, found in *B. Bava Qamma* 9a, is *not* applicable: Two brothers partitioned their father's estate. One took land and the other took money. A creditor of the deceased father came and seized land for the payment of the debt. If the brother who took the land seeks a new partition of the estate, the brother who took the money is fully within his rights to reply: "You chose to take the land for your part of the estate (with the implied condition) that if it were seized for the debt you would not be reimbursed by me. And I took the money (with the implied condition) that if it were stolen I would not be reimbursed by you." Money has an advantage over real property in that it cannot be seized for a debt,[2] and real property has an advantage over money in that it cannot be stolen. One may prefer one sort of advantage over another. But here in this loan case we have money and a pledge; one is not preferable to the other: both may be stolen, neither may be seized for a debt. Therefore one cannot raise the defense against Reuben that he took his share with full knowledge of possible untoward eventualities.

This entire legal argument rests on the assumption that the bishop

5

does not customarily deny or confiscate the debts or pledges of the Jews. The division of assets was therefore not made with any doubt concerning the soundness of the debt; and the bishop's action constitutes an uncommon sort of calamity which one would not have thought to provide against by an appropriate stipulation at the time of the division. However, if the bishop customarily *did* deny or confiscate debts or pledges from other Jews, and Reuben knew of this and did not protect himself with the appropriate stipulation for seeking a new apportionment from his former partners, he has, in the words of *B. Kethuboth* 93a, bought something without examining it beforehand. He entered into the division with doubt as to the soundness of the debt and cannot retract from his agreement, as any purchaser, who enters into a contract without satisfying his doubts about the item to be purchased, cannot retract. We learn this rule in *B. Gittin* 30a. There it is held that if one loans money to a priest (Cohen) or a Levite . . . on the condition that the loan is to be repaid from the proceeds of a sale of produce which that priest or Levite would receive as his lawful dues (tithes, heave offerings), this is a lawful transaction.[3] The rule is amplified by the provision that, if he—the lender—desired to retract, he may not do so; this provision against retraction applies to the lender since the loan itself involved an element of doubt on the lender's part as to whether, for example, the priest would live to receive the dues in question. The priest may retract his consent to the transaction since the priest has not yet delivered anything to the lender which the lender physically handled. (The payment of money is not the crucial element in the case of movable property; physical acquisition of the goods, even symbolically, is. The lender is perceived as a purchaser of the priestly dues; therefore he has to make an appropriate formal acquisition to complete the transaction. As long as this has not taken place, there may be rescission by the priest. The lender does not have the same right since the element of doubt arises on his side; and, as noted, no formal acquisition was effected.)[4]

Now one may argue that the Talmud, *B. Bava Qamma* 8b, in any case, holds that if A sold a field to B without warranty of title, and the title to the field came into dispute before B *took possession of it,* B can retract. Therefore, though the lender has—in the case of the priest—made the loan with this element in doubt as to his future rights to repayment, he should be able to retract as well, as long as he had not physically taken possession of the goods. Why, then, does the Talmud assert that he *cannot* retract? This argument is laid to rest because in the case of the purchase of the field the assumption is that money had not yet changed hands. The payment of the price effects the sale of real property, which is not the case with movables. Thus the element of possession becomes crucial because that property is to be acquired *by possession.*[5] (Three consecutive and undisturbed years of possession [or crop seasons] acquire land.) We are therefore given to understand that, once the possession has matured, one is obligated eventually to pay the money price for the field even though the title may be disputed after the possession has matured into acquisition.

## Notes and References

1. *Shulhan Arukh, Hoshen Mishpat* 232:1; Maimonides, *Hilkhoth Mekhirah* 15:1-2.
2. In talmudic law only real property was subject to distraint for debt, even if sold to a third party. Cf. Herzog, *Main Institutions of Jewish Law,* vol. 1, pp. 4 f., 386; Menahem Elon, "Execution," *Encyclopaedia Judaica,* vol. 6, cols. 1007-20. The *Encyclopaedia Judaica* will be abbreviated *E.J.* hereafter.
3. A lay Israelite may not consume the priest's dues; he must sell them to another priest.
4. Maimonides, *Hilkhoth Mekhirah* 3:4.
5. The money is not delivered right away. Possession ripens into ownership, and the price is due once ownership has matured. Cf. Menahem Elon, "Hazakah," *E.J.,* vol. 7, cols. 1515-22.
   See *Encyclopedia Talmudit,* vol. 1, cols. 137, 162; Gulak, *Yesode Hamishpat Haivri,* vol. 1, p. 63; vol. 2, p. 156; vol. 4, p. 97.

# R. Moses Maimonides

No. 105        A partnership made through an agent

*Decision:* An agreement of a partnership binds all members of the partnership even when the contract was negotiated by only one of them on behalf of them all.

---

*May our master instruct us* in the matter of a group of partners dealing in silk in Fostat and a group of partners dealing in silk in Al Mahallah. Some of the partners in the latter city came to open a shop close to the existing shop in the former city—to drive the price of silk down and to injure the existing shop thereby. The partners in Fostat sought to make a partnership with the newcomers so that there would be one silk outlet in Fostat and one in Al Mahallah. . . . The method of arranging their partnership was as follows: one of the partners in Fostat went to the other city and drew up the document of partnership on behalf of his partners in Fostat and stayed on in the shop in Al Mahallah. A man from the other city came to Fostat and drew up (a similar) document of partnership. The assets of the two shops were not combined. . . . May our master teach us if this is a legal partnership or not? His reward will be doubled from Heaven.

*Answer:* The partnership is legal and binding on all parties since all of them knew of it and agreed to it. Moses has written.*

## Notes and References

* *Shulhan Arukh, Hoshen Mishpat* 176, 182.

# R. Moses Maimonides

No. 223        A change in currency

*Decision:* A debt contracted in a particular currency is to be repaid in the same currency if at all possible, and, if that is not possible, it is to be repaid in full value in the currency in use.

---

*Question:* What would our lord say in the matter of a man who owed another man coin of a particular coinage current at the time of the loan? Sometime later one coinage was changed for another (as the standard currency) which was worth less (per unit of metal) than the former currency. Is the debtor legally required to repay in the actual original currency of the loan or in the coinage current at the time of the demand for payment?

*Answer:* If he had a debt with this man for a specific coinage, it is proper to say to the debtor, "Repay me in the very same coin, if it is available," or, if it is not, "Repay me its worth now in the other coin."

This rule is not really like the rule in respect to a coin which has been raised or lowered (in weight of metal), or which they (the government) have exchanged for another of greater or lesser (weight in metal). This latter case is discussed in *B. Bava Qamma* 97b. (The point at issue is not the new *value* of the currency, but its change in name or identity.) The rule for the case under notice appears in *B. Kethuboth* 110b, where it is held that if one produces a note of indebtedness against another, which note is executed in Babylonia, one satisfies the debt with Babylonian coin; if it is executed in the land of Israel, one satisfies the debt with coins of Israel. This is the talmudic proof that one is obligated to return the coinage he has borrowed, not another coinage. However, if that coinage is no longer available, as we have said, then we determine how much it is worth now, according to the current coinage;

and he would repay with that currency in that amount. And Moses has written.*

# Notes and References

\* Maimonides, *Hilkhoth Malveh Veloveh* 17:9; *Shulhan Arukh, Hoshen Mishpat* 74:7 and 227:18.

See also Y.Z. Kehanah, "Shinnui Erekh Hamatbe'a Bemishpat Haivri," *Sinai,* vol. 25 (1949); Benjamin Rabinowitz-Teomim, *Hukkat Mishpat,* pp. 34 f.

# R. Solomon b. Adret

Sec. 4, No. 2    Partnership for an illegal act

*Decision:* A partner who stole goods and placed them with the assets of the partnership, which suffered economic loss due to the partner's theft, may not seek to have the other partner bear a portion of the loss. It is self-evident that the articles of partnership are framed for the purpose of lawful trade only, and a partnership for unlawful purposes is a nullity since no one can be "agent for an illegal act."

---

*You asked:* Reuben and Simon were partners in business, sharing equally profits and losses. Reuben went and stole something and suffered a loss because of the theft. Now he is claiming that Simon (as his partner) should bear his proper portion of the loss. And Simon replies that he is not obliged to give anything because there can be no lawful agency for an illegal act.

*Answer:* Simon bears no obligation for several reasons. First, out of hand one may say that they did not form a partnership for thievery and robbery, that Simon did not become "an accomplice of brigandage." Moreover, they stated explicitly (in the document of partnership): "for their work and their business."

Further: Even if Simon said to Reuben, "Go and steal, and I shall repay you for any loss you suffer thereby," Simon has not lawfully obliged himself, because Reuben is not his agent for an illegal act (there can be no such agency, *B. Qiddushin* 42b).[1] Wherein would Simon be obligated?

Even though Simon enjoys some benefit from the theft, he would be free of obligations because Simon may say, "I am pleased to use and enjoy something that is possessed lawfully; I am not pleased to use and enjoy something possessed unlawfully." This is as we find in the Talmud, *B. Nedarim* 35a, where the case is that a man declares, in the form of a vow, that this loaf of bread is forbidden to a particular

11

person. The man thereupon gives the forbidden loaf to that particular person as a gift. The question becomes: Which one, giver or receiver, has misused forbidden property? The receiver may assert that he is pleased to use and enjoy something he possesses through lawful means but is not pleased to use and enjoy something possessed unlawfully.[2]

## Notes and References

1. *Shulhan Arukh, Hoshen Mishpat* 182:1, gloss, and 177:5, and commentaries thereto.
2. Cf. also *Shulhan Arukh, Hoshen Mishpat* 176:12, gloss; and Menahem Alon's article "Contract," *E.J.*, vol. 5, cols. 923-33.

See also M. Zilberg *Kakh Darko Shel Talmud* (Jerusalem, 1962), pp. 75 f.; *Torah Temimah* to Exod. 21:2; Wahrhaftig, "Illegal Contracts according to the Halakhah" (Hebrew), *Sinai*, vol. 62 (1968), pp. 242-51; *Encyclopedia Talmudit*, vol. 1, cols. 338 ff.

# R. Solomon b. Adret

Sec. 4, No. 125    An obligation implied on the basis of
                   commercial custom

*Decision:* Since it is established that mercantile custom in a particular
locale provides that a person introducing customers into a shop is
entitled to a fee, plaintiff is entitled to that fee.

---

*You asked:* Reuben brought non-Jewish friends to Simon's shop. They
bought garments from Simon. Reuben has demanded that Simon give
him a wage—because shopkeepers customarily pay a reward to those
who bring in customers. Simon replies he has no obligation to do this
because he made no agreement to do this, the custom of shopkeepers
notwithstanding. With whom is the law?

*Answer:* The law is with Reuben, the claimant. Since the shopkeepers
follow this custom, if anyone does bring customers to a shop, such an
act, though not covered in a prior contract or agreement, is seen as if it
were explicitly covered in a prior contract or agreement. (Clearly) it is
for the purpose of receiving payment that one becomes involved with
the shopkeeper's work, brings him profit, and improves his business.
The general rule is that whatever commercial usage the majority of the
community customarily follows, though not provided for formally in
contracts, etc., is seen to be *as if it were* so provided. Similarly, in the
Talmud (*B. Bava Mezia* 104a)[1] we find that the talmudic authorities
term this "interpretation of ordinary speech." . . .

Where people give rewards for the return of their lost property, even
though the person returning the property does so without suffering any
economic loss as regards his effort or his own work, he is biblically
bound to give a reward. (This is so even though the biblical rule re-
quiring one to return lost property might possibly be performed gratis,
cf. Deut. 22:1.) This rule holds good even if the owner of the lost
property was under a vow to receive no benefit from the returner of the

13

property. In this case, if the returner did not in fact wish to accept the reward, the owner of the property has to donate the reward to some sacred purpose (i.e., some charity which supports a religious endeavor). This is as is mentioned in the Talmud, *B. Nedarim* 33a.[2] . . .

Moreover, what is the difference between the case of one who becomes involved with another's land without permission to do so, and cultivates and improves it, and this case of one who becomes involved with another's business, and improves it, where in fact rewards are customarily given for this? (The man who improved the other man's land is entitled to a reward for his labor!)[3]

## Notes and References

1. *Shulhan Arukh, Hoshen Mishpat* 42:15 and 61:5.
2. Maimonides, *Commentary to the Mishnah; B. Nedarim* 33a and the Commentary *Nimmuke Joseph* ad loc.
3. *Shulhan Arukh, Hoshen Mishpat* 204:4, gloss; Elon, "Minhag," *E.J.,* vol. 12, cols. 4-25.

See also Jacob Rabinowitz's article in *Tarbiz,* vol. 22, pp. 193-195; Gulak, *Yesode Hamishpat Haivri,* vol. 1, p. 28; *Encyclopedia Talmudit,* vol. 11, cols. 53 ff.

# R. Isaac b. Sheshet Perfet

No. 261    Details of a partnership

*Decision:* An opinion withheld in the absence of sufficient facts; historical obiter dicta.

---

*You asked further* about a company that was formed and at the time of its formation each partner contributed capital to it according to his means. After a few days, two of the partners took complete charge and peremptorily assumed authority, heaped (gratuitous) insult and reprimand upon the other partners, drove them out, and struck their names from the charter. The partnership has fallen apart, and because of the stormy situation only three of the partners (remain in the company).

Presently the ousted partners wanted to return to the partnership and to seek an accounting of it. Are they able to force the partnership to render an account either with or without their return to it? Are the others (i.e., those who took control) able to prevent them (from getting their accounting)?

*Answer:* Because you paid too much attention to fancy rhetoric, you did not give sufficient exposition of your problem—how and why did those partners leave the partnership: Under duress? Voluntarily? Under the rules of the partnership? Unlawfully? You also did not let me know what the rules of the partnership are. I am surprised how two partners could force out the others in such a way that (including those two) only three of the original partners remained, and the majority of the partnership no longer remains intact—and (yet) all the assets of the partnership remained with the two or three, for them to deal with as they wish. How is it possible that this was their intent (when they left the group)? So explain your question more fully, let me know the exact provisions of partnership, and I shall answer you. . . .

. . . If my answer has been delayed overlong, do not be surprised because I have been simply swamped with bales of mail from foreign parts, from inquirers who have framed their questions on various

15

matters with precision. Also, after the holidays, when I got around to answering you, I could not find a student copyist because serious students—even when they are not at study—are all occupied in preparing their own comments and glosses on the talmudic treatise we are currently examining. I prefer not to take them from their work.

Because so much time has elapsed (since you wrote), in order to put an end to my embarrassment, which rested on me with the weight of Mount Tabor (cf. Jer. 46:18), I have myself taken the trouble to make the fair copy.

## Notes and References

See *Shulhan Arukh, Hoshen Mishpat* 176; Gulak, *Yesode Hamishpat Haivri*, sec. 2, p. 192; Herzog, *Main Institutions of Jewish Law.*

# R. Asher b. Yehiel

Sec. 100, No. 9    An agent's commission

*Decision:* An agent for the sale of real estate is not entitled to the customary agent's fee if the seller is unwilling to sell to the purchaser whom the agent presented as a potential purchaser.

---

*And you asked* concerning the matter of Simon, who was acting as an agent for Reuben in the sale of Reuben's house. Simon went to Levi, and Levi (presumably through Simon's salesmanship) agreed to buy it. As matters turned out, Reuben did not want to sell to Levi because he (Reuben) said that he (Levi) was his enemy; he sold the house to someone else. Now Simon is claiming an agent's fee from Reuben.

*Answer:* I do not know by virtue of what Reuben has an obligation to Simon. There is not even an oath between them (to bind them contractually). When Reuben said to Simon, "Be an agent to sell my house," he (Simon) did go and speak with Levi; but Reuben did not want to sell it to Levi. This agency became a nullity. Since afterward Reuben sold to another, and Simon was not an agent in that transaction, why should Reuben give Simon anything?

It is everyday practice that there may be several agents working on one transaction, an agent to speak with Levi, and another to speak with Judah. Whichever agent closes the deal is entitled to the agent's fee. At times the seller sells to Zebulun himself! He does not pay any agent's fee in that case. It is quite plain that agents and marriage brokers receive nothing if a deal is closed without (their) good offices. Certainly, if this is a case of someone who saw the agent (conferring with Levi) and said that Levi was his enemy and he (therefore) did not wish to sell to him and afterwards he *did* sell to him, there is deception and he *must* give him an agent's fee. But in the case under notice he is not to give him anything. This is somewhat like the talmudic case (*B. Bava Qamma* 115b) in which Rav inquired of Rabbi (Yehudah Hanasi). The situation is that A and B both own donkeys. A's is worth half the price of B's. Now both animals are swept away in a swift current. A abandons his animal and saves B's more expensive one. The rule is that A may claim a wage for his efforts, but no compensation for the loss of his animal unless he made an agreement with B that B should indeed pay him for his lost donkey. Rav asked Rabbi what could be claimed as a wage if despite all efforts A could not save the animal and his own beast was swept away. Rabbi said that this was not a very good question: the rescuer can clearly demand a fee for his effort (unsuccessful though it was) but not the price of his lost animal!

Here in the case under notice also, one would give some small fee to the agent for his effort in speaking on behalf of the principal,[1] but no fee for agency (which is a substantially larger sum). One cannot advance this argument: that in the Talmud the element which prevented the rescue of the animal was not due to the owner of the animal (it was an unavoidable circumstance) but, in the case under notice, the agent is performing the commission of the seller, and the element that prevented closing the deal was in fact due to the seller—therefore the seller should give an agent's fee. This (reluctance on the part of the seller) is not properly termed a "prevention"—a negligent act by the seller (he had his good reason for not selling)! If Levi was his enemy, Levi appeared to him to be a "lurking lion" (cf. *B. Bava Mezia* 101b); and he did not want Levi to be named as the owner of his (Reuben's) property.

Moreover, the cases are not at all alike! In the talmudic case the man lost his own animal in order to save the other man's animal. But here the agent lost nothing (except a bit of time)!

Some of my teachers compare the matter of marriage brokers' fees to the talmudic case of the ferryboat (*B. Bava Qamma* 116a) in which a man, fleeing from prison, came to the boatman and said, "Here's a dinar—take me across the river."[2] The dinar is far more than the normal fare. Since the man did not say, "Here's a dinar *for your fee ...*," he need not pay more than the normal fare, despite his reference to a dinar. The man can claim that he spoke of the dinar only as a jest. So, too, with marriage brokers; their fees are kept to customary norms, even though large fees may be stipulated.[3]

## Notes and References

1. Cf. Maimonides, *Hilkhoth Gezelah* 12:4.
2. *Shulhan Arukh, Hoshen Mishpat* 264:7, gloss and commentators ad loc.
3. *Shulhan Arukh, Hoshen Mishpat* 185:6; Gulak, *Yesode Hamishpat Haivri*, vol. 2, p. 198.

# R. Simon b. Zemah Duran

**Sec. 3, No. 174**   Agency: sharing profit and loss in a partnership

*Decision:* Under a contract of partnership providing for equal shares of loss or of profit for each partner and a wage for the entrepreneurial partner, the partners must share loss on the original stock in trade, which had to be sold at a loss, and they must share profit on goods purchased with proceeds from the original stock if the second lot of stock brings a profit.

---

*To Mostagenem. You asked:* Reuben gave Simon merchandise valued at one hundred gold pieces; they were to share profits and losses (in transactions with this merchandise) equally. Reuben also gave Simon the sum of six pieces of gold as a salary for his effort in the business.[1] Simon was to transport the goods to Spain. He could not get them to Spain; he had to sell off the goods at a loss. With the proceeds of the sale he bought other goods on which he *did* make a profit. All this occurred in the space of a year.

Now the entrepreneur (Simon) asks: must he bear half the loss of the original goods; and is he obligated to give half the profit on the second lot of merchandise to Reuben; and is Reuben obligated to pay Simon the six gold pieces stipulated as the salary for Simon's work?

*Answer:* The stipulation concerning the six gold pieces as payment for work and effort is lawful. This is in line with an ordinance of the rabbis (*B. Bavia Mezia* 104b)[2] concerning a partnership of this nature: the capital is deemed to be half deposit (for which the entrepreneur bears only very limited liability) and half loan (for which the entrepreneur bears greater liability). If they are to divide profits and losses equally, the entrepreneur must receive a salary so that his efforts on behalf of the investor, as regards the "deposit half," do not appear to be usurious benefit for the investor. Since the stipulation (for salary, in this case) was lawful, he is obligated to give the wage which was agreed upon, whether the enterprise prospered or not.

19

Whatever loss was sustained on the first lot of merchandise must be shared in equal proportion, according to law, because half the capital is deemed to be a loan (i.e., since Simon bears greater liability for the loan portion, it follows that he must assume "half the loss" corresponding to his liability for half the capital).

Simon is legally obliged to give Reuben a half-share in the profit from the second lot of merchandise, which he bought without the knowledge of Reuben—even though he (Simon) would have to bear any *losses* on it by himself. This is because he acquired the second lot of goods without the permission of his investing partner. This is the law for the entrepreneur who sustains a loss in a transaction he concluded without the permission of his investor: he bears the entire loss, even though he would have to share any profit on the transaction with the investor-partner. We may propound this on the basis of *B. Bava Qamma* 102b: If one gives money to another for the purpose of purchasing wheat and barley is purchased: If it declines in price, he bears the loss; if it appreciates, the profit is shared. Maimonides wrote this in chapter 5 of his volume on the laws of agency and partnership.

## Notes and References

1. Maimonides, *Hilkhoth Sheluhim* 6:2; Haim Cohn's article "Usury," *E.J.*, vol. 16, cols. 27-33, particularly the sections dealing with the *heter iska.*
2. *B. Bava Bathra* 70b.
   On agency, see Nahum Rakover, "Agency," *E.J.*, vol. 2, cols. 349-354. See also Maimonides, *Hilkhoth Sheluhim*, chap. 1; *Shulhan Arukh, Hoshen Mishpat* 182; Gulak, *Yesode Hamishpat Haivri*, sec. 1, pp. 42 ff.; Herzog, *Main Institutions of Jewish Law* (on agency); Rakover, "Al Kelal Sheluho shel Adam Kemoto Bedine Mammonot," *Sinai*, vol. 63, pp. 56-80; Wahrhaftig, *Dine Avodah Bemishpat Haivri.*

# R. Simon b. Zemah Duran

**Sec. 1, No. 171**   Mutual responsibility of partners

*Decision:* A creditor may seek satisfaction of a debt from whichever member of a partnership can be contacted for such satisfaction; however, if all members of a partnership can be contacted, each is liable for a portion of the total debt.

---

*You asked:* Reuben sold a quantity of merchandise on credit to two brothers who were in partnership in a particular craft. The goods were required for that craft. When the time came for payment, the partners convinced him to wait a while longer and to sell them another quantity of merchandise required for their craft, also on credit. (The agreement was) that Reuben should wait and they would pay him both billings together at the stipulated time (for payment on the second delivery). He had delivered the first lot of merchandise to the elder brother-partner. The second lot was delivered to the younger, in the presence of the elder.

Reuben is now claiming his due from the younger brother, because the elder brother cannot be reached. The younger brother has charge over the household (i.e., affairs) of the absent brother. The younger brother does not want to pay him. Let us know the law in this matter.

*Answer:* The law is straightforward in this: the younger brother is liable for both debts, his and the elder brother's. This is explicitly provided in the Palestinian Talmud (*Shevuoth,* chap. 5, halakhah 1): In the case of a denial of a debt, noted in Leviticus 5:24, the rule excludes from a specific penalty one who denies that a debt is owed to one partner because the debt is owed to both partners (the debtor owes both partners and a denial of debt to only one of them is not a culpable act). R. Jose, in the Talmud, ad loc, propounded that if two (partners) borrowed from one creditor (and a sale on credit bears some resemblance to a loan), even though the document evidencing the transaction does not specifically state that the debtors are guarantors and sureties for each other (they are deemed to be so). Alfasi cites this rule in his epitome of the B. Talmud, *Shevuoth*, chap. 5.[1]

The inference follows clearly for our present case. Since one of them, in the presence of the other (i.e., the partners), purchased the merchandise which is necessary for the partnership, the other partner is a surety, and the creditor may sue either partner for the whole of the debt. This is what Maimonides wrote (*Hilkhoth Malveh Veloveh*, chap. 5) . . . If one of two partners incurred a debt for the purposes of the partnership, both partners are sureties for each other, even though this suretyship is not explicitly inscribed in the note. This rule also appears in *Tur, Hoshen Mishpat* 77, cited from a responsum of Rabbenu Asher (sec. 73, no. 12).[2]

This part of the matter is clear. However, one may take a more detailed look at the liability of the one partner. In terms of legal theory, does the obligation arise from a concept of agency for the other partner or from a concept of surety? Rashi, in his comments to *B. Bava Mezia* 34b, considers the case of partners who borrowed an ox, which was (then) stolen from them. Borrowers are liable for theft; but only one of the partners paid anything to the owner of the ox. The thief was later found. Ordinarily the thief would have to pay double the value of the ox to the borrowers. However, only *one* of the borrowers paid the owner *half* the value of the ox, which portion was, of course, his equal share of the partnership's liability. The question then becomes whether or not that one partner is entitled to half the *double payment* because he paid half the value. Rashi remarks that we could argue that the one partner should get half the double payment for having paid half the partnership's liability. It would appear, therefore, that a partner would bear only *half* the liability of the partnership, contrary to the rule of the Palestinian Talmud, which makes each partner liable for the whole of the liability of the partnership! Nahmanides resolves this problem so that it is no problem at all. He does so as follows: The obligation of the second partner is solely on the ground of suretyship. As long as the second partner (in the case of the borrowed ox) has funds to meet his half of the obligation, the first partner need only pay half to the owner of the ox. However, if the second partner does not have such funds, the first partner has to meet the liability under the law of suretyship, as the Palestinian Talmud requires.

However, Nahmanides's opinion does not yield anything relevant for the case under notice. Since the one partner is not available to answer a suit for the debt, Reuben can collect from the younger brother.

(Nahmanides assumes that *both* partners were available.) How much the more does Nahmanides's opinion have no necessary bearing on this case since Maimonides, in *Hilkhoth Malveh Veloveh,* chap. 25, lays down that the creditor may collect from whichever one of the two sureties he wishes. Although Nahmanides takes issue with this, Rabbenu Asher agreed with Maimonides that, one may sue either one of them, even though each individual could meet the obligation himself.

## Notes and References

1. Cf. also *Tur, Hoshen Mishpat* 77.
2. See also *Responsa of Joseph Colon,* sec. 183.

   See *Tur, Hoshen Mishpat* 77, 176; Gulak, *Yesode Hamishpat Haivri,* p. 192; Shmuel Dov Revital, "Partnership," *E.J.,* vol. 13, cols, 149-155; Elon, "Suretyship," *E.J.,* vol. 15, cols. 523-529.

# R. Meir b. Baruch of Rothenburg

**No. 125**  Labor law—retraction of a dismissal made in anger

*Decision:* Dismissal of an employee requires legal formality and form; moreover, a teacher is engaged for a child's education, which a father has no lawful power to impair, and, further, a teacher is not an ordinary workman who enjoys specific rights in regard to termination of employment, inasmuch as time lost in educating the young can never be made up. Therefore, the dismissal of a tutor during an angry outburst of the pupil's father is not lawful and binding despite the tutor's insistence to the contrary.

---

*Question:* (You) asked . . . about Reuben, who hired a tutor for his son for a year. During that time Reuben became angry with the tutor and told him: "Get out. I want to hire another tutor. You go do what you can!" After a short while Reuben regretted his action and wanted the tutor to remain. The tutor stood firm against returning. Is this case of dismissal like the talmudic case of remission of a slave's price (*B. Kiddushin* 16a) which implies that oral remission of a debt is valid in itself and does not require a confirming formal act of acquisition to validate it (thus the dismissal by word of mouth is binding)?[1]

*Answer:* It appears that this obligation is not dissolved by mere word of mouth. The proof of this comes in the same talmudic discussion in *Kiddushin* 16a in reference to a Hebrew slave. There is an objection raised to the necessity for a deed of manumission when freeing a Hebrew slave; which necessity is clearly stated in the Mishnah. Why could not one merely go to two witnesses and say to the slave, in their presence, "Go." Since this oral dismissal of the Hebrew slave is not valid, it is deduced that his body is owned by the master, and consequently the slave does not repossess his body by the master's oral dismissal (unlike an oral remission of an ordinary debt, which is legal). The same rule is good in the case under notice because an employee is

24

(for some purposes!) analogous to a Hebrew slave (cf. *B. Bava Mezia* 10a).[2]

Further: Since he hired the tutor for the *son*, the tutor is *already* under an obligation to teach the son; and the father has neither right nor power to cancel the *tutor's* obligation to provide such instruction for the son because we may bestow a right which benefits a minor child, not one which obligates or disadvantages a minor child. Proof for this point is in the *Tosefta, Kethuboth* 10:2: If a man undertook to support the minor daughter of his wife, and that child broke some of his possessions and caused him damage, he is not allowed to deduct the cost of the damage from the cost of her support. One acts for a minor's benefit, not otherwise. Moreover, there is proof for this from the *Tosefta, Kethuboth* 13:1 which holds that if one undertook to give money to the betrothed husband of one's minor daughter, and does not make good on that undertaking, the court compels the betrothed husband either to enter into nuptials with the girl, i.e., fulfill his obligation to marry, or to free the girl with a proper bill of divorcement. We again act to the advantage of a minor, i.e., to get her married or to get her divorced, but in no case to let her remain betrothed to a man who would keep her in that equivocal condition ad infinitum.

However, R. Eliezer b. Joel Halevi and R. Joel Halevi decided that a tutor is not an ordinary workman who could quit his day-labor job even if the day is only half gone.[3] The resignation of a tutor is perceived like a matter of immediate and irretrievable loss, and he has neither right nor power to break his contract (to teach). . . . Meir b. Baruch.

## Notes and References

1. Cf. Maimonides, *Hilkhoth Mekhirah* 5:11; *Shulhan Arukh, Hoshen Mishpat* 241:2.
2. The idea is that the Jewish workman is analogous to the Jewish slave, owned by a Jewish master, as long as the workman does not take advantage of his right to quit the job. The notion that the body of the workman is "owned" by the employer is severely challenged; cf. *Shulhan Arukh, Hoshen Mishpat* 333:8; the Shakh commentary, note 47; and *Tosafoth, B. Kiddushin* 17a.
3. Cf. *B. Bava Mezia* 10a; Maimonides, *Hilkhoth Sekhiruth* 9:4; *Shulhan Arukh* 333:3, 8, and commentaries thereto.

See also *Hilkhoth Mordecai* to the beginning of chap. 6 of *Bava Mezia; Responsa of Solomon b. Adret,* no. 873; *R. Jeruham, Netiv,* 29, sec. 3; *Responsa of David ibn Zimra,* sec. 1, no. 88; *Responsa of Joseph Di Trani, Yoreh Deah,* no. 50; Wahrhaftig , *Dine Avodah Bemishpat Haivri,* vol. 2, pp. 543 f.

# R. Solomon b. Adret

**Sec. 5, No. 229**    Hire of a tutor

---

*Decision:* The plaintiff, a tutor, may not demand the huge sum of money the father of his pupil vowed to pay in order to secure a suitable tutor for his son since the sum did not represent an actual offer of a wage, but rather an expression of the lengths to which the father would go to find a suitable person.

---

*You asked:* In the matter of the wealthy man who swore to hire a tutor for his son, (even if he had to pay) ten pounds (to do so).

*The answer:* My opinion inclines thus: From the aspect of the oath he swore, he is not obligated (to pay the rather large amount; the tutor eventually heard of the father's extravagant offer and wanted to claim the ten-pound stipend. The father, of course, had struck a bargain with him for far less). As long as he hired a suitable tutor (it is well) because this man took no oath to hire the most learned tutor he could hire. All vows are construed according to the intention (of those who make them—not according to the possible implications of their particular phrasing, *B. Nedarim* 55b). And certainly if this man had found a suitable tutor for his son for less than ten pounds, *and* he found another tutor who was a mature scholar of high standing at the rabbinical college, he would not raise the wage offered because the early stages of a child's education can be as well and as properly supervised by one who has not achieved the distinction of the rabbinate. . . . This man only intended to engage one who was suitable (for the task). This is similar to what we find in *B. Bava Qamma* 80a concerning the woman who took an oath that she would not refuse an offer of marriage. Since unsuitable suitors presented themselves, seeking to hold her to the literal meaning of the oath, the judges ruled that clearly the oath applied only to men who were proper prospective husbands. How much the more (was the intent of the father's oath for someone who was qualified, not someone of scholarly reputation) if (as is the case) he did engage a competent and careful tutor (not an eminent sage!).[1]

This tutor wishes to act improperly, and he approaches the father with sly tricks—because he heard of his oath—and practices deceit! This tutor is dishonest because he was engaged for less than ten pounds but now reasons that he has the father completely at his mercy (because of the oath) and "he has done that which is not right" (cf. Ezek. 18:18).[2]

Even if this tutor did not retract (his claim), if then the father acquired the services of one of his own relatives to instruct the boy, gratis, the father is not bound at all by his oath, provided the relative is qualified to teach. The father did not swear to seek out a learned Jewish sage, but (simply) someone qualified to teach his son, as we have said.

Moreover, there are many whose pedagogic technique in teaching Torah (is their strong point), and one may well learn more from them than from men whose scholarship is far greater! Since this (tutor) is fit, proper, competent, careful, and suitably trained—though there may be another who is more learned—the father has discharged his vow (by hiring him at a suitable wage).

However, if a father dismisses one tutor before he has engaged a second tutor, this constitutes, possibly, a prohibited act, because the father has an immediate and absolute obligation to provide for his son's education: and a tutor is present (to continue the instruction—the present tutor cannot be discharged until there is another to take his place, otherwise there would be an unlawful cessation of learning). This is similar to Rova's opinion in the Talmud (*B. Rosh Hashanah* 6a): If one has vowed to contribute to a charity, he must do so immediately (the needy are already present and waiting for his gift!). How much the more is the immediacy crucial in the area of education, for cessation from learning, even for a short time, represents an irreparable loss.[3]

## Notes and References

1. Cf. *B. Bava Bathra* 21a and *B. Gittin* 36a.
2. Cf. also *B. Shevuoth* 31a.
3. Cf. *Shulhan Arukh, Yoreh Deah* 219:2

# R. Simon b. Zemah Duran

**Sec. 2, No. 174**   The liability of an expert who gives an opinion gratis

*Decision:* An expert who provides his professional opinion in his field gratis is not liable for damage resulting from the incorrectness of that opinion. *Obiter dicta:* A nonexpert is liable for opinions which he represents to be expert, whether or not he takes a fee; an expert is liable when he takes a fee for an opinion which proves to be incorrect.

---

*You asked:* Reuben bought a bag of gold dust from a gentile and showed it to a (Jewish) goldsmith. He said: "See if this is pure gold, without dross. If it is pure, I shall give you half the profit (from my dealings with it) as your honorarium." The goldsmith looked at it and said: "It appears to me to be pure gold, without dross. I have determined this from its weight." The buyer relied on this appraisal and purchased it under the impression that it was pure gold. When he smelted it, it turned out to be brass.

What is the law and legal reasoning here? Should the goldsmith be liable under the rule that holds an expert appraiser, who takes a fee for his appraisals, and upon whose opinion a purchaser would rely, liable? This rule appears in Maimonides's *Hilkhoth Sekhiruth* (chap. 10:5) in the matter of one who shows a coin to a banker, and the banker says it is sound coinage. The banker is liable for any loss incurred since he is considered an expert, takes payment for his expert opinion, and the buyer does rely on his opinion. The case under notice appears similar to the case contemplated in this rule.

*Answer:* The goldsmith is free of any liability. A professional expert incurs no liability for giving a professional opinion unless he takes an honorarium for it. Apparently, according to the language of the inquiry, you deem this goldsmith to be like "an expert who takes an honorarium," since he would get one-half the profit. This is wrong. If there is *no* profit, he would get nothing. He would take a remuneration when and as there is profit. He would not be liable unless there were a loss (on the transaction—which there clearly is); and when there is loss, he has no remuneration! The sort of remuneration that would carry with it the obligation to make good a loss incurred because of reliance on expert advice is the sort that is tendered the expert from the questioner's own pocket at the time he seeks the opinion. If the honorarium comes from the proceeds, *if any*, of the transaction contemplated, this is not "honorarium" within the scope of the rule.

Nahmanides wrote in this fashion concerning the money of minor orphans. And even though the inquirer places reliance upon the advisor (in this case—where there is nothing that would be properly termed remuneration), there is no liability (for the expert in this nonremuneration case). This is so because a plea of liability where there is no honorarium, according to the Talmud (*B. Bava Qamma* 99b), is only applicable to the nonexpert who is culpable even if he takes no remuneration (forasmuch as he offered expert advice which he was not qualified to give). According to Alfasi and Maimonides, the person advised (by a nonexpert) would have to declare, "I am relying on you." According to R. Isaac the Tosafist (*B. Bava Qamma* 100a), such a declaration is not necessary: the nonexpert is prima facie liable (in case of his faulty advice). However, the expert who gives professional advice gratis has no liability, even should the inquirer rely on his advice. The reason for this is that after all he is an expert; (in terms of his professional reputation) what else could he do (but give the best advice— even gratis)? Indeed because he *is* an expert, would he then be liable to bear the responsibilities of mankind (for free advice, given in good faith)?

When the expert does take an honorarium, he only does so because those who seek his counsel would rely on him, and he would be financially responsible for losses due to his advice. When a layman purports to give expert advice, even if he does not take an honorarium, that layman is liable under the law governing indirect causes of economic loss.* He had no business getting involved in a matter which he knew nothing about and concerning which people would trust him. However, the expert, whom people consult, and who gives his professional opinion gratis, has not acted wrongfully or negligently if his advice was in error. Also this goldsmith, according to the inquiry, has explained why he gave the opinion he did: he was sure on the basis of weight that the material was gold. He gave his best opinion. If the material turns out to be brass, he is not liable. This appears to be the strict law.

If there is a local custom governing such matters, they should follow the customary practice. . . .

## Notes and References

\* Cf. *Encyclopedia Talmudit*, vol. 6, col. 461.

See M. Silberg, *Kakh Darko Shel Talmud*, p. 111. This work has been translated by Ben Zion Bokser, under the title *Talmudic Law and the Modern State* (New York: Burning Bush Press, 1973). Compare the ruling of Israel Chief Justice Agranat on the matter of an expert's responsibility for his opinion, 5 *Israel Law Reports* at 1317.

# R. Meir Halevi Abulafia

No. 276    Interpretation of a contract

*Decision:* Minor grammatical anomalies in a document do not render the document nugatory, as would major anomalies that significantly alter the meaning or implication of the document.

---

*You asked:* Reuben had two buildings, one inside the other (presumably one behind the other, one facing the road and another one behind it). There was an access path from the public roadway to both houses. They always used to enter the courtyard of the inner house by way of a room (courtyard? covered hallway?) of the outer house. Sometimes they used to enter the inner house by way of the upper story over the room (courtyard?) by a ladder (staircase?) at the side of the public roadway. Reuben gave Hanoch, his son, a part of the outer building. At the time he sold Hanoch the inner building, and both Reuben and Leah, his wife, indited a bill of sale for Hanoch as follows: "We have sold this with its entrances and exits . . . ." After a while Reuben and Leah took up residence elsewhere. And they left Hanoch with the outer building. Hanoch died. Afterwards, Reuben died. Hanoch's children came and sought to claim from Reuben's heirs the access through the outer building to the courtyard of the inner building which their father had acquired on the strength of the bill of sale in which was written, "its entrances and exits." Reuben's heirs pleaded that Hanoch's heirs had no such access because the entrances and exits mentioned in the document refer only to the entrances and exits which are for the building (itself) and the upper story at the side of the public roadway.

You wanted to be set right on the matter *and* to recall the language of the bill of sale in which the feminine noun "sale" is used. However, this feminine noun is immediately followed with the words "its entrances and its exits" having the possessive endings couched in the masculine! Grammatically the noun for sale should be followed by possessives in the feminine in order to agree with the noun for "sale."

You wanted to know if errors of this sort are significant in the construction of documents.

*Answer:* Thus we have seen: Were it not that the "entrances and exits"—mentioned in the bill of sale—were couched in *plural*, it would have been proper to say that Reuben had sold only the second-story entryway, which is open to the public road, because there are there an open doorway and a permanent ladder for entering and leaving. But with the phrasing in the plural, it is clear that the bill of sale refers to two entrances. "Entrances and exits" do not refer grammatically to the noun "sale" but to the masculine noun "house" which is used shortly before the noun "sale" in the document. There is no copyist's error.

Moreover, if you should argue that the two masculine endings on the nouns do refer to the feminine form "sale," the document is not voided by this since the context demonstrates that he sold it to him with "entrances and exits" (which are clearly plural) and those two nouns need only be supplied with the appropriate feminine possessive endings! What (genuine problem) is there (then) if he mentioned the words whose antecedent is "sale" with masculine endings or feminine endings? We do not take such matters into account in the construction of documents except when the word in question may reasonably be interpreted in more than one way; or when the word in question has a significant bearing on the validity and scope or the rights of the litigant. Our talmudic basis is *B. Kethuboth* 83b, where it is held that, if one produces a document in court for the purpose of getting possession of property or money in someone else's possession (he having a reasonable title to it), "the one presenting the document has the disadvantage." That is to say, such a document will be given the narrowest possible interpretation. However, when it is clear that the doubtful language cannot reasonably be interpreted in more than one way, even though the language is not precise, the unclarity does not nullify the intent of the document.*

## Notes and References

*Shulhan Arukh, Hoshen Mishpat 142:5-9.*

# BOOK 3

## Real property
## landlord and tenant
## responsibilities of neighbors
## privacy

THIS SECTION consists of eight texts, all dealing with various rules concerning real property in Jewish law.

The first case concerns the knowledge that a purchaser is presumed to have concerning the condition of real property he is buying. The second case takes up a matter of servitude, or easement, in which neighbors quarrel over the rather pedestrian but nonetheless serious problem of who is to pay for the draining of a cesspool.

Another case reveals the sort of quarrel which could develop in the aftermath of anti-Jewish persecution or expulsion. A tenant was unable to enjoy the property he rented for the full term of the lease because he had to flee the community. The question arose concerning a possible refund of the rent money or a possible extension of the lease gratis.

There is a case concerning an attempt of a lessee to renege on an oral promise to quit the leased property. The matter involved the technical requirements for the lawful breaking of the lease.

The sale of mortgaged property and the possible eviction of the mortgagee figure in another case. The point at issue becomes the rights conferred on the purchaser by the sale.

A purchase of real property today does not necessarily give the purchaser exclusive rights to use and enjoy the substrata of the earth beneath his property. Mineral rights may be excluded from the sale. One case here deals specifically with the ownership of subsurface land.

Finally, there is a case on a potential threat to privacy. This matter reflects a strong traditional desire to protect and preserve the private nature of residences, a point of view that was difficult to maintain in the crowded conditions of medieval towns and cities.

S.M.P.

# R. Joseph ibn Migash

No. 51    An exchange of real property; defects in the property

---

*Decision:* The purchaser of a building is presumed to have knowledge of manifest structural defects in said building at the time of the purchase, and this knowledge bars his suit for rescission. Purchaser need not accept vendor's offer to repair the structure; further decided that a nonstructural defect or servitude, if repaired or removed by the vendor, is not ground for rescission.

---

*You asked* concerning Reuben, who exchanged buildings for a field with Simon. After a while Simon complained that there were defects in the buildings, which he had not known of. Reuben said to him, "I informed you of them, you considered the matter and accepted the transaction." Simon rejoined, "It was not that way at all!" Reuben pleaded further, "Even if things are as you say, that I did not fully inform you of defects, I shall repair these defects and remove them."

*Answer:* If the aforementioned defects are apparent, readily seen by anyone entering the building, and if Reuben has witnesses who can attest that Simon did in fact enter the property at the time of the exchange or afterward, Simon's assertion that he had no knowledge of them is unacceptable. If (on the other hand) the defects are not apparent—or if they are, but there is no one who can attest that he (Simon) did in fact enter the buildings at the time of the exchange or afterwards—Simon is to take an oath that he did not enter the buildings, did not see the defects, and had no knowledge of them whatsoever; and the exchange is null and void.

Surely one has to consider carefully what Reuben said: "Although you did not know of the defects, I shall repair and remove them . . . . " If the aforementioned defects are not in the buildings themselves (i.e., internal, structural defects) but arise because of external factors, as, for example, a sewer canal that passed through them, or a water pipe that spurts on them, or a right of easement possessed by one of the neighbors in respect to their walls, and the like, then the removal of these (external) defects in the property would leave the buildings safe and sound. There would be no new structural work on the buildings themselves. Therefore, it follows that once those (nonstructural) defects are removed the exchange would be valid and proper.

If the defects in the building are structural, as, for example, the walls appear to be well founded but are in fact only leaning on each other, or the building itself seemed sound but in fact had deteriorated, even if Reuben rebuilt the walls to eliminate the deterioration and would renovate the blighted building, the exchange is null and void. This is so because the building *and* the repair work were not part of the original building before the exchange, but the renovation is after the fact of the exchange. It is as if the property were a wholly new phenomenon, "new faces" in the talmudic idiom (*B. Kethuboth* 112b), and the exchange was not effected for such new or repaired property.

But surely a defect that exists because of excavations in the ground (i.e., something that undermines the building), e.g., cisterns or ditches or caves, although (if these are eliminated) one would not assert the concept of a "new phenomenon" (to nullify the contract) because the building and the walls remain just as they were at the time of the exchange, no change having been made in *them*, nevertheless, because the defect involved the buildings themselves as structures, even if one were now to install a marble flooring (to correct the weakness in the ground underneath the building), which any reasonable man would say is a complete job of repair, the exchange is null and void ab initio since the buildings were not really sound at the time of the contract.

Proof for this line of argument comes from *B. Kethuboth* 74b: If a man formally betrothed a woman on condition that she had no physical blemishes, but she did in fact have such blemishes at the time of the formal betrothal, and then this woman went to a physician to have the blemishes cured, and the physician did effect a cure, the betrothal is void. How much more is the contract invalid here, where the structures themselves were defective at the time of the exchange and could only be put right by the additional work now, after the exchange.[1] (In the betrothal case, the marriage was yet to be completed by the nuptial ceremony; the man and the woman did not live as a married couple on the strength of the formal betrothal alone.) But surely talmudic authority has asserted that if the man betrothed the woman on condition that *he* had no physical blemishes, but he did in fact have them, the betrothal is and remains *valid*. The reason behind this is given in the

35

Talmud (*B. Kethuboth* 75a) by R. Simeon b. Lakish: it is better (so women supposedly say!) to be married than to remain single. However, this latter line of reasoning is traditionally restricted to the specific case of a man with blemishes, and no inference can be drawn from it.

In regard to the talmudic principle of "here it is,"[2] in which a creditor claims one hundred *zuz* from the debtor and the debtor responds, "here are fifty *zuzim* and they are yours" (i.e., I have not used them; they are your property in every respect), (we know that) in this case the debtor is not obliged to take an oath[3] in respect to the remainder of the creditor's claim. (In biblical law, the debtor's partial admission of a money debt requires such an oath; a full denial of the debt requires none. The declaration "here it is" carries with it exemption from this oath as well because part of the money is deemed to be in the creditor's possession by virtue of the declaration and the other part of the creditor's claim is not acknowledged: in effect, a full denial! There is an erroneous interpretation concerning renovation of real property that is worth mentioning in the case under notice.) If the debtor is free from the obligation of an oath concerning the remainder of the creditor's claim, why does the Talmud require special reference to a biblical verse to support excuse from the oath when the claim concerns *real property*? Any case of real property is a case of "here it is," i.e., if a debtor presents (some) of the real property in response to the claim, such property is clearly fixed, immovable (and in the creditor's possession), a true case of "here it is" (so there should be no oath to begin with). The Talmud supplies the answer that the biblical verse is required in support of exemption where the debtor has excavated, dug ditches, etc. (i.e., the character of the land has been altered). One expositor asserts that the talmudic answer means that, since money as such is not claimed in this case, rather a restoration of the land, filling in ditches, etc., the very same earth that was removed from the property is to be used in restoring the ground. (Presumably, too, no oath is to be required when the suit is for return of a parcel of land exactly as it was and the debtor can of course return only "part" of the land.) This interpretation is in error. The reason the verse is required proceeds rather from the idea that when the land was excavated the principle of "here it is" (and the exemption from oath under it) no longer really applied since this was no longer the "same land" that the creditor is claiming (a matter of excavated versus nonexcavated land). That is to say: One *is obligated* to take an oath in regard to a claim concerning movable property if one, as a debtor, acknowledged only part of his creditor's claim; the biblical verse permits (extension of) the ruling, that

36

there is no such obligatory oath, to the case of a debtor acknowledging only "part of the *land*" claimed by the creditor, due to the debtor's excavations, ditches, etc.[4] (since the notion of "here it is" does not provide exemption in this particular case).

## Notes and References

1. Maimonides, *Hilkhoth Ishut* 7:9.
2. Maimonides, *Hilkhoth To'en Venitan* 1:3. This is a complex matter. Ordinarily a debtor who denies part of the creditor's claim must swear an oath concerning the remainder. This oath is part of biblical law. Here, however, no explicit denial is made. The debtor says he has only a certain part of the creditor's money, goods, etc., and "here it is"—you have them. The debtor is assumed to assert that the goods are in the creditor's possession, and they are, from any point of view, the creditor's property. The assertion is legally taken to mean that the money, etc., is in fact in the creditor's possession. The debtor says nothing about the remainder. In effect the debtor denies the whole of a debt in the sum he specified. No biblical oath is required for full denial of debt. The talmudic authorities, however, did require an oath in a case of full denial. The debtor is assumed to be returning the very same goods, etc., he borrowed.
3. Oaths may be "rabbinical," that is to say, instituted by early rabbinic jurists for situations not covered by biblical oaths, which are clearly specified in certain biblical laws. See the article by Haim Cohen, "Oaths," *E.J.*, vol. 12, cols. 1298-1302.
4. *B. Shevuoth* 49b; *Shulhan Arukh, Hoshen Mishpat* 232:5 and commentators thereto. See also Herzog, *Main Institutions of Jewish Law*, vol. 2, pp. 124-28. See as well Gulak, *Yesode Hamishpat Haivri*, vol. 1, p. 63.

# R. Joseph ibn Migash

**No. 132** Joint responsibility of neighbors

*Decision:* Defendant liable to assist in removal of refuse water from plaintiff's cesspool, which water collected there because of a lawful servitude. Defendant's right was limited to the passage of the water in plaintiff's property, not to its collection there.

---

*Question:* The sewage effluent from Reuben's building flowed through a pipe to Simon's building, where it settled in an underground cistern which also held the sewage from Simon's building. When the cistern had become full and it was necessary to empty it, Simon said to Reuben, "Share the expenses of emptying the cistern with me." Reuben said, "I have no such obligation; since it is my right to have my sewage pass into the cistern, you may do with it what you wish!"

May our master instruct us and may Heaven doubly reward him.

*Answer:* Reuben is legally obligated[1] to empty the cistern at Simon's building since, if it is not emptied, Simon will have no place for his sewage to collect. The essence of the servitude[2] in Simon's property is that the sewage should *pass through* Simon's property into the cistern, not that it should go and remain in his building!

The talmudic proof for this is found in *B. Bava Mezia* 108a, where it is held that people living on high ground are obligated to assist people living in a valley to clear obstructions from sewers or storm drains which carry off rainwater to prevent its backing up on the high ground and flooding the town there. On this basis the "upper resident" (Reuben) is bound to assist the "lower resident" (Simon) to clear the water so that the former's sewage will be able to flow again into the cistern, since we have already said that Reuben's servitude in Simon's property is specifically to put his sewage there in the cistern, not to burden Simon with it!

## Notes and References

1. *Shulhan Arukh, Hoshen Mishpat* 161:6.
2. See *Black's Law Dictionary*, 4th rev. ed. (St. Paul: West Publishing Co., 1968), p. 1535. A servitude is defined as a charge or burden resting upon one estate for the benefit or advantage of another. The concept comes from Roman law; one estate is termed dominant and the other, servient. The institution is similar to the easement of the common law.

# R. Eliezer b. Nathan

**No. 98**  A lease of a building, abandonment of the leased property due to persecution, an argument over the rent money

*Decision:* A tenant who vacated leased premises under duress, i.e., persecution, should lawfully occupy the premises free of charge for a period of time equal to the period of time during which he was prevented from enjoying his leasehold. However, whereas this particular instance of duress was a calamity suffered by the community as a whole, both landlord and tenant are to share the loss—in enjoyment and in rental—equally.

---

*Question:* I, Eliezer, respond to my dear and beloved kinsman Eliezer b. Samson[1] on the matter of Reuben, who leased a building from Simon for two years and paid the full rental in advance. While the term of the lease was running, the Jews of that town had to flee in fear of their lives. Reuben abandoned the building he had rented. When the Jews returned to the community, Reuben also came back. He wanted Simon to refund to him the portion of the rent for the time he had to abandon the building. Simon replied, "My building was before you (i.e., it was at your disposal)—you leased it, and I am not going to refund anything."

*Answer:* It appears to me that Reuben's plea is well founded and unassailable, since the case was occasioned by force majeure affecting the community in general, and on the basis of the talmudic source you adduced (*B. Bava Mezia* 105b): If one leased a field and (the crop) was eaten by locusts or blighted (by natural causes), and that calamity was general in the area,[2] the lessee may deduct from the agreed-upon rental[3] (in proportion to the extent of the damage; the rental being in any case a portion of the crop). In this rule there is no distinction made as to when the rental was paid: at the beginning or the end of the term of the lease. The phrasing of the talmudic rule "may deduct" and not "he shall return the rental" (does not imply a distinction in this law as

39

between prepaid rental and rental paid at the end of the term of lease but rather) represents the more common situation, which is that rental is paid at the conclusion of the term of the lease. But if the rent were prepaid, there is still no difference in the law on this matter.

The case is also well supported by your citation of the rule on the charter of a ship, *B. Bava Mezia* 79a. That is: if one chartered a ship and she sank "half-way along the route" (i.e., after completing part of the voyage), R. Nathan, the talmudic authority, asserted that if the charterer gave the money already he shall not take any of it back. This view follows the assumption of the ensuing talmudic discussion of *B. Bava Mezia* 79a, which proceeds on the footing that a specific ship—now at the bottom—and a specific cargo—taken to be wine—are involved. Since the charterer is no longer able to produce the specific cargo of wine—now lost at sea—the owner of the vessel is not to return the money he took for the charter. If the charterer *were* able to present the specific cargo of wine, R. Nathan would agree that the owner would either have to produce the specific ship or return the money! So also, since Reuben has said, "You should let me complete the full term of my lease" (i.e., Reuben wants to use Simon's building rent free for a period equal to the time he had to leave the town because of the general danger to the Jewish community). Simon is legally bound to let him complete the term of the lease (i.e., as with the ship, if one party to the contract is able to fulfill his obligation, the other must discharge his obligation or return the rental, etc.).

However, the talmudic rule is, after all, phrased "deduct from the rental" and not "the entire rental."[4] Since there was a general calamity, the loss falls on both of them, each one bearing half the loss. Thus, Simon is to permit Reuben to use the building rent free for a period equal to half the time that he had to abandon it, and Reuben is to absorb the other half of the loss himself.

You might possibly reason that this phrasing "deduct from" points to the argument that, as a rule, locusts or other blight do not destroy the entire crop; and what remains after the lessee's expenses, in this case, of a blighted field, belongs to the lessor as his rental; and the lessor would simply deduct the remainder of the rent (i.e., the destroyed crop) for the lessee and absorb the loss. Therefore, you opine, we have the phrasing "deduct from the rental" (i.e., deduct the destroyed crop) and it turns out that the lessee has, in effect, lost nothing. So Reuben, the lessee, should lose nothing. Really one cannot raise such an argument because the general calamity was a common misfortune and so the loss is to be borne by both of them.

Further, even if one could argue that the lessee is to lose nothing in the case of a blighted field, here in the case of a building, it is logical that the lessee should lose half of his rental. In the field case the bad luck befell the lessor's field, because most of it was blighted, and the bad luck was not really the lessee's. But here in the building case, one may say that the misfortune affected them both: the buildings were abandoned and the people in temporary exile. Since this is a case of bad luck befalling *both* of them, the loss is to be divided equally, as the Talmud, *B. Bava Mezia* 106a, provides: If something has occurred because of someone's misfortune, his bad luck, he is to bear the loss (since both parties are involved in a common instance of ill fortune, both have responsibilities).

And further: In the field case the lessee could say to the lessor, "Would the field have escaped blight had it been in your care or some other tenant's care?" (Clearly not.) But here the lessor *can* say to the lessee, "If *you* had not leased my building, perhaps one of the people who were *not* expelled from the town would have rented it—since, in fact, some few of the Jewish community were permitted to remain— and I would have lost nothing." Since this point gives rise to some doubt (after all, the lessee's ill luck was as much involved as the lessor's), they are to bear the loss jointly.[5]

## Notes and References

1. This rabbi was a kinsman of R. Eliezer b. Nathan and one of the significant figures in Franco-German Jewry of the twelfth century. He lived in Cologne. See Agus, *The Heroic Age of Franco-German Jewry* (New York: Yeshiva University, 1969).
2. *Shulhan Arukh, Hoshen Mishpat* 332:1.
3. The Talmud assumes the rental to be a portion of the crop. The measurements used in the talmudic and rabbinic discussions are compared with modern equivalents in the entry "Weights and Measures" in the *E.J.* The article has several contributors.
4. The question of sharing the loss received some learned attention over the years. The gist of the problem is, as we shall see, that not all the Jews had to flee, so it is possible that the lessor could have had a tenant who was permitted to stay in the town and who thereby could have enjoyed all of the rental term. If this possibility is granted, why should the lessor, who is in possession of the money, be required to give up half of it? It is only possible that the lessor and lessee really shared in ill luck, and thus the losses. The lessee certainly had bad luck; the lessor could, perhaps, have had a more permanent tenant. However, the opinion is also expressed that in cases of doubt the loss should be equally shared. Yet the matter

of doubt is taken to mean that the traditional law on a particular point is not clearly resolved; only in that situation is the loss to be shared equally. In this case the law is clear that the money (or property) is in the lawful possession of one party and could remain with that party; it was a lawful rental. Thus the lessor need not return anything. Both on the basis of fact and on the basis of law, it is at least arguable that the loss is to be borne by the lessee. Cf. *Shulhan Arukh, Hoshen Mishpat* 322:1, and *Kizoth Hahoshen* commentary thereto.

5. Herzog, *Main Institutions of Jewish Law*, vol. 2, pp. 255-75.

See also *Encyclopedia Talmudit*, vol. 1, col. 162; Gulak, *Yesode Hamishpat Haivri*, vol. 1, pp. 57-60, 143-45; vol. 2, pp. 163-67, and note 17 to p. 166.

# R. Isaac b. Sheshet Perfet

No. 510    The lawful method of breaking a lease

*Decision:* The lessee of real property may refuse to honor an oral agreement to return the leased property to the lessor for refund of the rental. Only the appropriate legal formalities, duly observed, can render the agreement binding.

---

(To) Montalban.

*Question:* This honorable gentleman, holding the royal appointment as bailee[1] of the Jews in Montalban, asked me about the quarrel between two Jews, to wit: One of them leased land to the other for a specified time. The lease was executed with proper formalities of a document and a formal, symbolic act of transfer. The lessee paid the rental before he took possession of the property—(which property he leased) in order to construct a building necessary for that land. . . . Afterwards the lessee wanted the lessor to give him the land. The lessor put him off and expressed the view that he wanted to get out of the lease. When the lessee saw that the lessor did not wish to go through with the contract of lease, he said to the lessor, in the presence of witnesses, "Since you do not want to go through with the contract of lease, return my money." The lessor does indeed wish to return the money to the lessee, as (formerly) the lessee had asserted his desire to get it back—*in the presence of witnesses.* The lessee now says that he does not want his money, rather he wants the land which was let to him. He has retracted what he said to the lessor in the presence of witnesses and (now) says that, because there was no formal, legal act of transfer to validate the voiding of the contract of lease, he is not about to relinquish his rights under that contract of lease, even though he said in the presence of witnesses that he would do so. With whom is the law?

*My answer* is that the law is on the side of the lessee. Since he lawfully acquired the land for the term of the lease—both by the requisite

43

formal transfer and by the payment of the rental, it is *his* for that term and he cannot remove himself from it (i.e., the contract) by words alone—even words spoken in the presence of witnesses. (He can only retract by means of a formal, symbolic act of transfer validating the retraction.) The contract of lease is deemed to be a sale for a specified term, *B. Bava Mezia* 56b.

Even in the case of one who has pledged land to his creditor for a specified term, without further stipulation, *and* the commercial custom of the district is that the creditor need not vacate the pledged property during the term of the pledge—even though the debtor pays off the loan—the Talmud holds (*B. Bava Mezia* 67b) that if the creditor said to the debtor during the term of the pledge, "If you pay me off I shall vacate the pledged land," the creditor has said nothing of legal effect— he may retract such a statement, *unless* (the statement) is validated by the proper symbolic act of transfer.[2] How much the more is this symbolic validation crucial here (in the case of the creditor) because (his removal from the pledged land) is not a matter of mercantile custom, but the case is that he explicitly stipulated in the document, and confirmed the document by symbolic transfer, that he would not vacate the pledged land for the term of the pledge. Therefore, when he asserted afterwards that he would vacate, the validating formalities were required.

Furthermore, in that talmudic case (i.e., the creditor-debtor-pledged land case), the creditor did not take possession of the land except by virtue of the *loan*—and even so (when the loan is repaid early) he is not to vacate the pledged land, except after the legal formalities of symbolic transfer! How much more does it follow here in the case under notice—which is a contract of lease, a *sale* for a definite term, that since he leased the land for the term with the formal symbolic transfer, and the land is acquired from then on, even though he did not take possession of it, the retraction has no force, without the symbolic formality of transfer. . . . Isaac b. Sheshet.

## Notes and References

1. See Baer, *History of the Jews in Christian Spain,* and Abraham Hershman, *Rabbi Isaac b. Sheshet Perfet and His Times* (New York: Jewish Theological Seminary, 1943).
2. Cf. Maimonides, *Hilkhoth Malveh Veloveh* 7:3.

The background for the law on this matter is provided in the following works: Karo's *Beth Joseph* to *Tur, Hoshen Mishpat,* no. 312, and *Shulhan Arukh, Hoshen Mishpat* 312:1; Gulak, *Leheker Toledot Hamishpat Haivri Betekufat Hatalmud,* first sec., pp. 43 ff.; Maimonides, *Hilkhoth Mekhirah* 1:1; *Shulhan Arukh, Hoshen Mishpat* 189:1; Benjamin Rabinowitz-Teomim, *Hukkat Mishpat,* pp. 2 and 166.

Herzog's *Main Institutions of Jewish Law* also affords background for this matter.

# R. Solomon b. Simon Duran

**No. 439**   Sale of mortgaged property

*Decision:* In a case in which the owner of mortgaged real estate sold it during the term of the mortgage, and the possibility arose that the new landlord might evict the mortgagee, it is decided that the new landlord enjoys no such right. The new landlord has no greater rights than the former one.

---

*You asked further:* If one mortgages a building for a period of ten years and, during the term of the mortgage, sells the property to another party, can the purchaser evict the mortgagee?

*Answer:* The sale does not destroy any rights created by the lease and the mortgage. This is explicitly provided in *B. Bava Mezia* 101b; if a person sold, bequeathed, or deeded land by gift, a lessee in possession of the property will not have his leasehold voided by this sale, bequest, or gift.* The lessee can say to the new owner, "You have no more legal power (to put me off this land) than the man through whose power you acquired the land (the vendor, grantor, etc.). If the one who gave, bequeathed, or sold it to you was not able to remove me—how could you do so, you whose rights derive from him? You have no more power than he!" Maimonides wrote this (*Hilkhoth Sekhiruth*, chap. 6) that the legal power of the purchaser, heir, or donee is no greater than that of the vendor, etc.

There is no difference here between lease and landed security for a loan (i.e., mortgage) because the underlying principle is the same: the purchaser, etc., has no greater right than the one from whom his own rights derive. And the owner of the courtyard was not able to dispossess the lender, who was in possession of his landed security, nor is one who purchases from that owner so entitled to do.

Although gentile law runs contrary to this, it is forbidden for us (in this sort of case) to follow their law!

## Notes and References

* See also *B. Bava Mezia* 67b; *Shulhan Arukh, Yoreh Deah* 172; Maimonides, *Hilkhoth Malveh Veloveh*, chap. 7; Herzog, *Main Institutions of Jewish Law*; Gulak, *Yesode Hamishpat Haivri*, vol. 1, p. 164.

# R. Meir Halevi Abulafia

**No. 272**  A wall between adjoining apartments

*Decision:* The thickness of a wall between neighboring landholders is in its entire thickness jointly possessed.

---

*You asked:* There was a wall which stood between the adjoining properties of Reuben and Simon. They owned the wall jointly. One of them wanted to insert some beams into the wall from his side of it. To do this he wanted to pierce the wall completely in order to set the beams properly. The other one protests this action and insists that the hole can only extend to one half the wall's thickness. With whom is the law?

*Thus we have seen:* The law is with the partner who wishes to insert the beams into the full thickness of the wall since their individual portions of wall are not limited to the part that faces their respective properties. The entire wall is jointly enjoyed. Imagine: if one of them wanted to reduce the thickness of the wall facing his property, the other could surely prevent him (from weakening the entire wall in this fashion). If you were to argue that each had rights only in the half of the wall facing his own property, how could one of them prevent the other from reducing the thickness on his *own* side? You learn therefore that the entire wall is held jointly. Therefore it is lawful for each to make use of the (entire) wall: provided that the beams do not project beyond the wall into the other partner's building. Thus is the law. . . . Meir b. R. Todros Halevi Abulafia.*

## Notes and References

*    *Shulhan Arukh, Hoshen Mishpat* 153:14, 157; Maimonides, *Hilkhoth Shekhenim*, chap. 3.

# R. Solomon b. Adret

Sec. 4, No. 143    Tunneling under another's property; a right to use
                   subsurface land

*Decision:* A title to land is deemed to extend from the bowels of the
earth outward; therefore a landlord may prevent excavation under his
property even if the excavation would in no way damage the surface
land or buildings on the surface.

*You asked:* About the matter of the caves which people customarily
excavate under their neighbor's buildings, which caves are dug into
subsurface rock and which excavations never endanger the buildings on
the surface. May the owner of the surface property restrain others from
digging under his land? Or would the neighbor who wants to excavate
be able to say: "What difference does this make to you? You should
have no fear that the land under your house would cave in because the
rocky stratum is solid and will not be weakened by excavation. And if
*you* wish to excavate a cistern tomorrow, my excavation will benefit
you—you will find one already dug! And if you are afraid that I shall
lay claim to some right in the subsurface land on the basis of unchallenged occupancy over a period of time (usucapion), register a demurral
with a court so that the period of *unchallenged* occupancy cannot run,
as in the Talmud" (*B. Bava Bathra* 21a).[1]

*The answer:* The law is with the owner of the surface property because
he legally owns his lands from the bowels of the earth to its surface.
How could anyone excavate it or use it against his wishes? The neighbor's claim that the owner could register a demurral, to allay any fear
of a future claim to an easement on the ground of occupancy, is no
solution. If this one should *occupy* the land, would it be necessary to
protest with him? (No, he would be a trespasser to begin with.)

The entire discussion in *Bava Bathra* alluded to is predicated on the
view that the *owner* of the land is using his property in such a manner
that harm may come to his neighbor's land when the neighbor might
build on it. But there was no permission given for one actually to make
use of his *neighbor's* land.

48

Put yourself into the situation: If we are considering a building that is not ordinarily leased, which is occupied against the wishes of the owner—could the squatter say to him: "What do you care? When you need the space I shall leave! If you are worried about my getting owner-ship through undisturbed occupancy—go raise a formal demurral (to preclude the ripening of such ownership)." This is assuredly not the law! Even according to the authority who holds that premises are better kept up through occupancy—even the occupancy of squatters, who have no obligation to pay rent. The matter (of upkeep and no contract to pay rent) clearly applies only when the squatter occupied the premises first (by some innocent inadvertence). Then there is no obligation to pay rent. (It does *not* apply in the face of the owner's refusal to let the squatter take up residence.)[2]

## Notes and References

1. See also *Shulhan Arukh, Hoshen Mishpat* 146:1 and 153, glosses.
2. See *Encyclopedia Talmudit*, vol. 12, cols. 2 f.

# R. Solomon b. Adret

**Sec. 1, No. 1144**    A window overlooking another's property

*Decision:* One neighbor may seek permanent injunction to halt an adjoining neighbor's attempt to construct a window overlooking the first neighbor's property, even though the construction represents only the potentiality of invasion of privacy.

---

*You asked:* Reuben wishes to open (i.e., construct) a window overlooking a neighbor's property at a place which would presently cause him no harm or embarrassment by reason of loss of privacy. (The rabbinic legal concept literally means "harm of sight," but the idea involved is a loss of privacy because one can peer from his window into the property, or into the dwelling, of someone else.) Simon complains that he could, in the near future, build on his own property and Reuben (i.e., his window—if constructed now) would cause a loss of privacy. At present there is no such harm involved if the window is constructed. The earlier authorities expressed two opinions in this matter.[1] You asked me to make a definite decision in the case—as to whether the law favors Reuben, who comes to construct the window, or Simon.

*The answer:* My decision is not definitive. However, I have it on the authority of R. Jonah Gerondi that he (Simon) would be able (lawfully) to restrain him (Reuben), since he does not desire to bring suit at a later time (i.e., after the window is installed), when he (Simon) would come to build (on his own property) and consequently would be subject to harm from Reuben by virtue of "his own arrows" (i.e., a presently lawful act done on one's own property—for instance, shooting an arrow—which may cause damage on to another's property).[2] He (R. Jonah) asserted this on the basis of the Palestinian Talmud's discussion of the principle that ruined buildings are ordinarily to be rebuilt. In this discussion it is noted that it is unlawful to construct doorways in buildings opposite ruins so that, when a ruined building is reconstructed, those who live in it would be deprived of privacy by the doorway of an opposing building. Therefore R. Jonah taught that a man may enjoin another from constructing a window which in future would destroy his privacy. (Presumably a building was constructed opposite the ruin even though the ruin was to be rebuilt; even a ruin to be rebuilt was viewed with an eye toward the privacy of its future inhabitants.)

This case also suggests the argument of Abaye and Rova in *B. Bava Bathra* 17b and 25b.[3] There Rova asserts that, where a man wishes to dig a pit close to his property line, his adjoining neighbor may prevent him; he may enjoin his neighbor even in respect to other causes of damage which do not constitute direct and immediate sources of harm. This accords with the majority rabbinic view (expressed there) that the one who is the potential cause of the damage must withdraw or stop the potential cause of harm. Even according to R. Jose, who takes issue with the majority and says that one need not remove *potential* causes of damage, e.g., one need not refrain from planting a tree near a property line because its roots will *eventually* damage a pit on the adjoining property, even so R. Jose agrees that in case of direct and immediate harm one may be enjoined from doing what will certainly damage the adjoining property. Rova's opinion is, therefore, that a *pit* dug close to a property line represents a direct and immediate danger to adjoining property and that work can be halted—even according to R. Jose. If all the items specified as potential dangers to adjoining property by the Mishnah (*B. Bava Bathra* 17a: construction of an oven, a cowshed, or a mill near a neighbor's wall—or under his loft) are taken as direct and immediate dangers to an adjoining property, the talmudic debates and counterarguments (24b) concerning the injunctions against potential damage to property may be deemed to reflect situations of clear and immediate harm—*even according to R. Jose.* Now even though the potential dangers of the window do not endamage property at the very moment of its construction as do, e.g., millstones or an oven which were in place before the neighbor built his wall,[4] yet since one *can* say that he wishes to avoid future litigation (one may stop the construction of the window).

Therefore, since one cannot place a potential cause of damage (near a neighbor's property) when that potential cause of damage is a direct and immediate one, and since *eventually* he has to remove it, the neighbor has no case based upon the prior existence or presence of this potential cause of harm.

Nonetheless, the law is established for us in the Talmud (*B. Bava Bathra* 59a) that we may compel people to abandon a dog-in-the-manger attitude, to desist from hampering one's neighbor in the peaceful enjoyment of his property, which enjoyment causes no annoyance, interference, or harm to anyone.[5] The Talmud asserts there that R. Zera holds that windows constructed within a space of four cubits from ground level (which windows afford a view of a neighbor's private property) are deemed to be protected by the legal assumption of *hazakah* (i.e., strength, which is to say, such a window is deemed to have been made with the knowledge and consent of the neighbor, and a neighbor not wishing to have a window constructed in such a place is able to raise an immediate protest against such a project. If he does not, the assumption is that he consents to the window's presence and waives his right to claim invasion of privacy because of the window). If the window were above four cubits from ground level, R. Zera[6] says that the assumption of *hazakah* does not apply and the neighbor has no right to prevent construction of such a window (because the window is too high for overlooking the neighboring property, the neighbor is not apprehensive about it and there is no need for protecting it by claiming *hazakah*).

Now R. Elai holds that a window above four cubits from ground level is *also* protected by *hazakah* and the neighbor may raise an initial protest (against such construction so that no *hazakah* can be established). R. Elai holds this view only because the neighbor might occasionally place a stool beneath the window and stand upon it to look out on the adjoining property. Thus if this sort of contingency could not arise, R. Elai agrees that no protest could be lodged against constructing the window because we do compel people to abandon a dog-in-the manger attitude—to stop annoying people in the peaceful enjoyment of their property.

In the case of the window, the reason one might construct it is because there would be no harm at all caused to anyone. Should the owner of the window come to prevent his neighbor from erecting a wall opposite the window, the owner of the window would have no such right because the window (which could not be used for spying on the neighbors) is not protected by *hazakah*. Since he does not (in future) suffer any impairment in the enjoyment of his property (i.e., if he wants to build that wall), why should he prevent him now (from constructing the window)?

However, here the situation is not the same (as in the case of the window discussed in the Talmud). If the one party should build on his property he is directly and immediately harmed by the (prior) act of the owner of the window. He would suffer harm (i.e., invasion of privacy) from the time he builds the house until the time he could sue the owner of the window, win his case, and have the window blocked. If he protests the construction of the window now, this is not unwarranted interference with the neighbor's peaceful enjoyment of his own property. It is reasonable behavior.

How much the more (is the window to be prevented) since rabbinic jurists have differed on the law concerning invasion of privacy as to whether or not (a window that could be used for peering at one's neighbors is protected by) *hazakah*. Perhaps a court will render a decision that it is so protected—even though it might cause no immediate harm (as in the present case)—and consequently the defendant (Simon) had always been obliged to raise an immediate protest. (And not having done so—he has waived his right to protest later.) Even if Reuben were willing to indite a binding declaration of acknowledgment that he waived all rights to his window when and as Simon should build on his (Simon's) property, we do not permit him to do this. This course of action would necessarily place an (unwarranted) duty on Simon to protect the document "from mice" (i.e., from loss and destruction). The talmudic authorities laid down that quittances are only indited for debtors (*B. Bava Bathra* 170b: if one has repaid part of a debt, a quittance is made out, but the creditor keeps the original note. It was felt that it was more just for the debtor to be responsible for keeping the quittance). The rule on quittances for debtors only is based on Proverbs 22:7, "The debtor is the slave to the creditor" (cf. *B. Bava Bathra* 171b), and on the idea that one (i.e., the debtor) should not enjoy (the wealth of the other, the creditor, if the creditor should lose the original note. Ergo, the quittance is kept by the debtor). If this consideration—or the particular debtor-creditor relationship—does not apply, which in the case under notice it assuredly does not, no quittance is indited (i.e., the owner of the window does not draw up a waiver of his rights).[7]

## Notes and References

1. *Shulhan Arukh, Hoshen Mishpat* 154:16; the differing views are those of Alfasi and ibn Migash, respectively; cf. *Tur, Hoshen Mishpat* 154 and *Beth Joseph* ad loc.
2. *B. Bava Bathra* 25b; Maimonides, *Hilkhoth Shekhenim* 10:5.
3. Cf. also Maimonides, *Hilkhoth Shekhenim* 10:7.
4. *B. Bava Bathra* 50b.
5. Maimonides, *Hilkhoth Shekhenim* 7:8; *Shulhan Arukh, Hoshen Mishpat* 153:8, gloss.
6. *B. Bava Bathra* 59a.
7. *Shulhan Arukh, Hoshen Mishpat* 154:16; Prof. Tedeschi in *Hapraklit*, no. 25, p. 282.

# BOOK 4

## Sale of movables
### sale of defective or damaged goods
### usury
### possession of movables

THERE ARE eight cases in this unit, and they deal with what is perhaps the most common form of contract: the contract of sale. Many Jews of the medieval period were in commerce; many of them were merchants. Even the Jews who engaged primarily in banking for a living were no doubt not reluctant to buy and sell merchandise when the opportunity to do so presented itself. Virtually anyone could be a merchant, given the opportunity.

The cases here concern the sale of movable property. One peculiarity of the traditional Jewish law on such matters has to be kept in mind: the importance of *qinyan*, the formal and legal acquisition of the goods through some specific act, for instance, pulling the item toward one, which legally makes the purchaser the new owner. The payment of a money price does not in itself transfer title to movable property; it does do so for real property. The act of *qinyan*, once performed, obligates the purchaser to pay the previously agreed upon price. This legal and formal acquisition was originally supposed to preclude the possibility of the vendor's negligence with the goods once he had received his money. Once the buyer has, as it were, taken possession, the goods are his; money changes hands later.

The matters covered in these texts include mistakes of fact, confusion about price, the discovery of defective or damaged goods, and even installment payments, all questions which are as alive today as they were five hundred or more years ago. Clearly the matter of warranty would play an important role in modern versions of these cases, but warranty as such is not discussed. There is, however, the unspoken assumption that goods offered for sale have to be in good and usable condition. Jewish law does prohibit false and misleading advertising and, of course, fraud.

One case deals with a situation in which a demand for full value of goods on credit was not held to be usurious. The goods had fallen in value and the purchaser attempted to return them. The vendor wanted an additional cash sum. The charging and paying of interest among Jews was roundly proscribed by Jewish law; the prohibitions were carried through in great detail and even extended to some aspects of sales on credit. There were, of course, some clever and lawful devices to permit an investor some return on capital, but these were very carefully regulated. The modern type of interest-bearing loan was prohibited.

The last case involves a matter of possession and ownership. Owing to the often precarious nature of life in the Middle Ages, people had to abandon property in case of fire, flood, or persecution. Presumably, they frequently despaired of ever seeing their abandoned possessions. What, then, of the person who rescues such property: thus a case of possession and ownership.

S.M.P.

# R. Meir b. Baruch of Rothenburg

**No. 258** A buyer's complaint: fraud or mistake of fact

*Decision:* The details and circumstance of a sale, e.g., price, clearly show in what manner the vendor represented the item to be sold; if the item was not, in fact, of the nature or quality represented by the vendor, rescission may be sought.

---

*Question:* Reuben raised a complaint against Simon: "You sold me something that was supposed to be gold.[1] Now I have broken the item and found it to be copper." Simon rejoins: "I made no vow to you (that it was gold), but I sold it to you in the same condition that I purchased it. If you take an oath that I vowed it was gold, I shall repay you." Moreover Simon says: "Give it back to me in good condition and I shall refund the sale price." Reuben cannot do this; he broke it and sold it (the pieces).

*Answer:* Even though Simon sold the item without specifying any particulars about it and did not say it was gold, since the external appearance of the item was of gold, and the purchase price indicates whether (or not) the item was presumed to be gold (the price apparently did so indicate), the sale was thus a transaction involving a mistake of fact.

Even though conditions and stipulations which one may have in mind when he enters a contract, which conditions are left undisclosed, have no legal effect, and Simon did *not* explicitly say that (he was selling the item) as gold, the matter (stands) as if he had done so. We are virtually in the position of witnesses to the fact that Reuben bought the item as a gold object. (Since the circumstances of the case, the price, etc., so clearly point to a sale of a golden object, it is as if Simon *did* explicitly stipulate that the object was gold, no matter that Simon said nothing explicit.)

This matter is analogous to the talmudic case (*B. Kethuboth* 97a) of the man who sold a field because he needed money right away for some

57

purpose, but it turned out that at the time the money was not required for that purpose. In that case, even though the field was sold without any specification of what the proceeds were to be used for, the contract was voided as a sale made under a mistake of fact.[2]

There are numerous situations in which it can be said "we are witnesses" (i.e., the circumstances are so clear and their meaning so compelling that we may be said, as it were, to have been witnesses that a particular condition or stipulation was in fact made). We say (moreover in these cases) that unspoken opinions or attitudes do have significance; and the matter is *as if* Simon had made an explicit statement about the gold content of the object (i.e., he did not have to *say* anything, the circumstances and the way he handled the transaction clearly imply that he was dealing in gold). There is no need to pursue this further.[3]

However, if Simon denies Reuben's claim and says: "I do not believe you when you say you found lead (*sic*) in the object," Simon should swear an oath that he did not know of the lead and he would be quit of any obligation. And if Simon would protest and say: "If you would have returned the object to me unbroken—as I sold it to you—I could have sold it again. Now that he (Reuben) has broken it, it is of no use to me—he has acted negligently with his own property." Such a claim of "negligence" is not good. How was Reuben to know that there were copper and lead in the object? If he had known, he would have returned the item unbroken.

Along this line, we have the talmudic case of *B. Bava Mezia* 42b concerning a guardian of orphans who purchased an ox with the orphans' money. The guardian put the ox into the charge of a stockman, a paid bailee. The ox, however, had no teeth, could not eat, and died. Ordinarily the stockman would be answerable for the death of the ox in these circumstances. However, if the orphans managed to get their money back from the seller and really suffered no loss, what then? The sale, after all, involved a mistake of fact concerning the health of the ox. The Talmud asks: Who then is the plaintiff if the orphans managed to recover their money? The Talmud asserts that the *original owner* of the ox is the plaintiff, since he surely knew at the outset that this mistake of fact could upset the sale later. He might sue the guardian, but the guardian was not under obligation to inform the seller of the ox's infirmity. The seller presumably already knew of it. The Talmud then proposes that the case involves a cattle broker as the seller, a man who buys and sells livestock and does not himself inspect the animals he deals in. Even such a cattle broker would have to return the orphans' money in this matter of a mistake of fact as to the animal's health. The guardian would not be liable because he could not have been expected to know of the ox's infirmity; he put the animal into a stockman's care. The broker, for his part, could swear an oath that he did not know of the animal's infirmity and recoup a portion of his loss from the stockman, who would not reimburse the full amount because he had a somewhat plausible defense in the first place: he fed all the animals in his charge and was not aware that this particular one had not eaten. Yet granted that the stockman was a paid bailee and should have known of the ox's infirmity (though he might argue the point), the guardian was under no obligation to know of the ox's infirmity. Thus it is also in the case under notice that Reuben had no duty to examine the object he bought, and he did not act negligently when he broke it.

Therefore if it is clear that Reuben found lead in the object, as he claims, there has been a sale with a mistake of fact and that sale may be rescinded.

## Notes and References

1. Irving Agus's monumental *Rabbi Meir of Rothenburg* (Philadelphia: Dropsie College, 1947) provides an excellent treatment of R. Meir's voluminous correspondence.

2. As a matter of fact, the talmudic rule is that the sale may be voided only if the vendor specifically stated that he sold the field because he was in need of money. Cf. Maimonides, *Hilkhoth Mekhirah* 11:8 f.; *Shulhan Arukh, Hoshen Mishpat* 207:3.

3. Cf. also Herzog, *Main Institutions of Jewish Law*, vol. 2, pp. 116 ff.

See also *Encyclopedia Talmudit*, vol. 2, col. 70; Benjamin Rabinowitz-Teomim, *Hukkat Mishpat*, p. 88, par. 7; Gulak, *Yesode Hamishpat Haivri*, vol. 1, p. 63; Herzog, *Main Institutions of Jewish Law*, vol. 2, pp. 116 ff.

# R. Meir b. Baruch of Rothenburg

No. 809   Confusion over a purchase price

*Decision:* A clearly understood specific price is an essential element in a contract of sale, without which rescission may be sought.

---

*I would ask you* to inform me concerning Reuben and Simon who have come to law against each other. Reuben said to Simon: "Sell me your cloak." Simon answered: "I shall give it to you for two coins." Reuben said: "I will only give you one coin."

Three weeks later Reuben came to Simon and said: "Give me your cloak." Simon gave it to him. Neither party mentioned the price. Two weeks later Simon came to Reuben and said: "Either give me two coins or give me my cloak." Reuben said to him: "I will give you one coin, because when I came to you I was under the impression—due to your silence—that you gave it to me for one coin."

Simon replied: "I was silent then because I thought you had agreed to my price!" . . .

*Answer:* It seems to me that Reuben's formal acquisition of the cloak (by means of pulling it toward himself when he took it from Simon) was done in error (i.e., was not legally binding) since Simon had never agreed to sell the cloak except at the price of two coins. When Simon gave the cloak to Reuben, in all likelihood, he gave it to him on the assumption of his first quoted price (two coins) being accepted. Anyone who advances the argument that perhaps Simon had mentally resolved to sell it for one coin is speculating in the realm of mental stipulations and reservations; and in this sort of situation such stipulations and reservations have no weight whatsoever.

A formal act of acquisition (of movable property) without the (prior) setting of a price effects no lawful acquisition of the property. In the case under notice, it is as if no price was set. Where in our legal tradition do we come to the conclusion that where a price has not been set there is no legal acquisition (despite performance of the requisite formal act of acquisition)? The Talmud, *B. Avodah Zarah* 71a, discusses the case of a Jew who is selling wine to an idolater. Now the traditional law is that wine which has been touched by an idolater (not to mention manufactured by him) is unfit for consumption or enjoyment by Jews; even the proceeds from the sale of such wine are assumed to have been used for, or dedicated to, some idol, all of which is totally repugnant to Jewish religious sensibilities and law. Now if the price for the wine has been set prior to the measuring out of the wine for the idolater, the purchase price is permitted to the Jew, i.e., the price, if set first, is part of the contract; if not set first, the idolater's contact with the wine precludes the right of the Jew to sell the wine and there is no sale. In our case under notice, as long as the seller has not agreed with the purchaser about a price, there is no transaction—just as there is no transaction in the case of the idolater and the wine. Thus the prior setting of price is crucial to the transaction.[1] (The same discussion in *Avodah Zarah* raises this point in reference to real property as well.)

Moreover, I say that if one pays only one coin for a cloak that is for sale at two coins, there could not possibly be more of a case of fraud regarding a price[2] (since the maximum allowable inconsistency between price and payment is one-sixth of the price—either as overpayment or underpayment; here the difference is one hundred percent). The sale may be rescinded. In the Talmud, *B. Bava Mezia* 49b, the point is made that, although the purchaser has only a limited time during which he may rescind a sale on the grounds of a fraudulent or excessively inflated price, the seller has no such time limit, according to R. Nahman.[3]

## Notes and References

1. See also Maimonides, *Hilkhoth Mekhirah* 8:7; *Shulhan Arukh, Hoshen Mishpat* 206:1.
2. Maimonides, *Hilkhoth Mekhirah* 12:4.
3. *Shulhan Arukh, Hoshen Mishpat* 227:7; *B. Bava Mezia* 50b. Cf. also Maimonides, *Hilkhoth Mekhirah* 20:1; *Shulhan Arukh, Hoshen Mishpat* 221; Herzog, *Main Institutions of Jewish Law,* col. 2, pp. 116 f.

See also Benjamin Rabinowitz-Teomim, *Hukkat Mishpat,* p. 13; Gulak, *Yesode Hamishpat Haivri,* col. 1, p. 63; Herzog, *Main Institutions of Jewish Law,* vol. 2, pp. 116 f.

# R. Asher b. Yehiel

Sec. 97, No. 1       Noncompliance with conditions concerning time
and place of installment payments

*Decided on appeal:* The purchaser who has stipulated, in a contract for
a sale of real property, that payments are to be made at specified times
and that if the purchaser is in default in one payment he shall forfeit all
monies already paid and the contract shall be null—is justifiably seen to
be in default if a payment is made to a third party who holds the said
contract and not to the seller directly. Payment to a third party does
not constitute payment.

---

*Question:* Leah sold a building to Simon. He gave her some of the
money immediately and he stipulated times for the rest of the
payment, with the condition that if he were to miss a single time for
payment all the money already paid would be deemed a gift and he
would have to return the building to her. The landlord whose property
adjoined Leah's building bought the building from the buyer (Simon)
and paid him the money he had given to her. When the time for the
next payment came, just prior to it, the adjoining landlord came and
gave the money to the notary with whom the bill of sale, with its
stipulations, had been deposited. The notary did not inform Leah that
he had the money until the stipulated time for the payment had passed,
whereupon Leah said she did not wish to accept the money. Since the
time for payment had passed, the money she already had from the
transaction was hers to keep; and the building reverted to her! The
adjoining landlord asserts that since he had given the money to the
notary he had fulfilled the stipulation. The matter was litigated; the
judges found for the adjoining landlord. Complaints (about these
judges) developed, and they sent the pleas of the parties and their
verdict to me (for review).

*Answer:* ... Even though these matters show in the main that Leah is (merely) seeking occasion to revoke the sale, I shall write your answers according to our rabbinic law—but, if there is some other custom in that city (which requires a resolution differing from rabbinic law), follow it.

We have learned in the Talmud (*B. Gittin* 74b) that if a man declares to his wife that she shall be divorced on the condition that she give him a specified sum of money within thirty days, if she does in fact give him the money she is divorced; if not, she is not divorced. The Talmud raises the point that this matter of fulfillment and nonfulfillment is too obvious to require mention. The rejoinder is that this "obvious" point is raised to forestall any argument that the condition was not a matter of genuine concern, but merely a device to encourage prompt payment. Thus it follows that if one sets a specific time for a payment of money the matter of the set time is an important and operative element of the contract (i.e., a condition going to its root). We do not say that if the payment is a bit overdue it does not matter, since the condition was merely to encourage promptness (not to demand it as part of the contract). Surely this matter of a fixed time for payment is serious; and, once the payment is overdue, the contract is null.

I have examined your letter carefully. You wrote that the condition was that he should pay *her* part of the money immediately; *her* implies to her and to no one else. As we have also learned in the section from *Gittin* cited above, if the man declares that she shall be divorced "on condition that you (the wife) give to me (the husband)" a specified sum of money and he *dies*, if the woman has in fact given the money to him before his death, she is not subject to levirate marriage; if not, she is subject to levirate marriage. She is not able to satisfy the condition by giving the money to one of her husband's heirs—that she not be subject to levirate marriage. The phrase "to me" implies to me and not to my heirs. Even according to Rabban Gamaliel, who holds that she *can* give the money to one of the heirs (thus satisfying the condition and freeing herself from the levirate obligation), because he reasons that "to me" also implies "to my heirs" (should he die): such a view applies only after the death of the man who leaves his legacy (including accounts receivable!) to his heirs. However, during his lifetime the man would want the money to come to himself—not to any others (and in the case under notice the seller is very much alive and able to act for herself). This is in line with the talmudic dictum, *B. Gittin* 29a, that a man, whose agent for accepting some article has fallen ill, may very well not want that agent to appoint another in his stead: "for a man does not wish his deposit to be in the possession of another" (whom he did not appoint).

Even if she did not use the specific wording that the money be given "to her," but they stipulated that the money was to be paid at a specific time, the condition governing payment has not been fulfilled if the money did not go to her personally. If he gave the money to someone else and said, "Take possession of this money for Leah"—in order to fulfill the condition—this is not the lawful payment under the contract. She is, after all, in the city, and he is able to give *her* the money. We learn from *B. Arakhin* 31b of the development of the law concerning the sale of a building in a walled city. Under biblical law, the seller could redeem the building by returning the price to the buyer within twelve months. After the twelve-month period the sale became final and absolute (see Leviticus 25:29 f.). Now it used to be that the buyer could hide himself on the last day of the twelve-month redemption period so that the seller could not redeem the property! Hillel ordained that the seller could deposit the redemption money with a court—or at the Temple treasury—and take possession of the building even if that meant breaking the door down! The buyer could pick up the redemption money when he wished. This ordinance is predicated on the circumstance that the buyer intentionally made himself unavailable; but, if he was available, it was (still) necessary to give the money to him (personally).

Simon also raises the argument that his part of the contract was fully discharged in that he (the neighbor?) gave the money to the notary for, if he (Simon?) had given all the money to him, the notary would have surrendered the document which had been deposited with him. Therefore: It is as if he had given the money to Leah (herself). On this point I say that if the notary had done this (surrendered the document) he would have done so unlawfully. He had no right to surrender the document until Leah was in possession of the money. Although Leah reposed confidence in him to hold the document, this is no reason (to hold) that she trusted him as a depositary for her money!

As for what you wrote: that the adjoining neighbor only need bring the money to the court which awarded him the property, this is incorrect. (The neighbor apparently was to deposit the purchase price with the court, since he had not, so it was held, acquired the land from Leah but, through the court, by exercise of the right of preemption enjoyed by an adjoining landholder.) The buyer is deemed the agent of the neighbor-preemptor, and all conditions which the buyer made are to be fulfilled by the neighbor-preemptor.

I have written an opinion in conformity with Jewish law. But if there is a custom in the city that, in sale of real property, delivery of the purchase price to the notary constitutes payment and the notary may forthwith surrender the document, as paid, to the buyer, even though the proceeds of the sale are not yet in the possession of the seller himself, this custom may set aside the traditional law as long as it is generally recognized in the city. We read in the Talmud (*Bava Mezia* 74a) that where merchants purchase large quantities of wine in barrels, leave them in the distributor's warehouse until needed, and put their personal seal on the barrels, "the seal effects formal and legal acquisition"—even without other traditional formalities of acquisition. Any (mode of) acquisition of movable goods which the merchants of the city customarily employ (as this one of placing one's seal on the barrel) is legally valid.[1] If it is so (that there is a specific custom governing sales of real property in the city), then Simon did not act negligently in that he (the neighbor?) gave the money to the notary. He fulfilled the condition. And in the same way, in regard to the decision you rendered as a court of three judges without the participation of one of the town elders, I say that you were procedurally correct according to Jewish law. However, if there is an ordinance in the city that no decision is to be rendered without the participation of one of the city elders with the court (of three),[2] the community is within its rights to depart from the regular procedural requirements of Jewish law and to institute an ordinance according to what they deem to be proper.[3] Asher b. Yehiel.

## Notes and References

1. Maimonides, *Hilkhoth Mekhirah* 7:6.
2. Cf. *B. Bava Bathra* 8b and Rabbenu Asher's case, sec. 78, no. 1.
3. Cf. also *Shulhan Arukh, Hoshen Mishpat* 190; *Shulhan Arukh, Yoreh Deah* 236, and the *Taz* commentary ad loc.; Gulak, *Yesode Hamishpat Haivri*, vol. 2, p. 107; Herzog, *Main Institutions of Jewish Law*, vol. 2, pp. 245, 266.

On the power of local ordinance: *Encyclopedia Talmudit*, vol. 3, col. 150; vol. 1, cols. 279-82; Isaac D. Gilat, "The Power of the Court to Stipulate against a Biblical Provision" (Hebrew), in *Bar-Ilan Yearbook*, nos. 7-8, pp. 117-32; Menahem Elon, "The Nature of Community Ordinances in Jewish Law" (Hebrew), in *Legal Studies in Memory of Abraham Rosenstiel*; Elon's "Takkanot" and "Takkanot Hakahal," *E.J.*, vol. 15, cols. 712-35; and the indispensable work of Louis Finkelstein, *Jewish Self-Government in the Middle Ages* (New York: Feldheim, 1964).

# R. Moses Maimonides

## No. 275    Sale of defective merchandise

*Decision:* Local mercantile custom concerning damaged goods is controlling in a suit for rescission, provided that purchaser states upon oath that he did not know of the flaw at the time of the purchase and did not use the item after he became aware of the flaw.

---

*Question:* What would you say . . . in the matter of Reuben who sold Simon a piece of linen cloth. Simon cut it (from the bolt) and inspected it completely. He then pondered it, settled on a price, and paid a portion of it. After a while he brought it to a clothing merchant(?). When Reuben attempted to get payment on the remainder of the price, Simon refused to pay and said, "The goods were not satisfactory." And Simon tried to force Reuben to take it back, without showing a specific defect and without alleging fraud (in the price). Is the sale legal or not; is it proper to return the goods or not? . . .

*Answer:* If the cloth shows some peculiarity in its substance, which the people of that place customarily classify as a defect in this sort of linen[1] and the purchaser pleads that he did not see it and had no knowledge of it—since he did not (yet) pay the (full) price of the linen— he has to take an oath prescribed by rabbinical ordinance (not the one required by biblical injunction). This oath is to be to the effect that he did not see the defect and it is to incorporate a statement that he did not make use of the linen after the defect became apparent and he did not renounce his legal remedies in respect to the flawed goods. Then he may return the goods to the vendor.[2] And Moses has written.

## Notes and References

1. Maimonides, *Hilkhoth Mekhirah* 15:5; cf. also 15:3.
2. *Shulhan Arukh, Hoshen Mishpat* 232:3, 6.
   See also Benjamin Rabinowitz-Teomim, *Hukkat Mishpat* pp. 90, 93; Gulak, *Yesode Hamishpat Haivri*, vol. 1, p. 63.

# R. Solomon b. Simon Duran

No. 476  A garment sold and found to be damaged

*Judicial guidance:* Reviewing the possible origin and causes of damage to an article and the legal implications of each possible cause in a suit concerning rescission of the sale of the damaged article.

---

*You asked further:* If one sells a garment and it turns out to be damaged, can one return it on the principle that the sale was made under a mistake of fact?

*Answer:* It seems that there are several possibilities involved here. If the garment was torn and sewn together, it may be manifest (in this case) that the sewing is the sort customarily found in the cloth of woolen garments from Italy, so that clearly the sewing was not done with the knowledge and consent of the purchaser; the sale may, of course, be rescinded. If the garment has holes in it, and if the holes appear to have been made with a knife, then, if the purchaser has already paid the price of the goods, he must bring proof that the holes were made while the garment was still in the possession of the vendor. If he has not yet paid for the garment, the purchaser should take an oath that the damage did not occur while the garment was in his possession and then return the garment and be quit of any responsibility. If the holes were made by mice—and this sort of damage is identifiable—cf. *B. Bekhoroth* 29b, the gnawing of mice is identifiable—it is the purchaser's responsibility to bring proof that the damage occurred while the goods were in possession of the vendor, whether the purchaser had paid or not. He does so whether or not he has paid the price because this damage is not the sort concerning which he could swear an oath that *he* had not done it, as he could with a rip in a sheet, etc.; and it is the sort of damage that could have occurred immediately after he (the purchaser) had gotten the garment; even if he had stored it away in a chest. Occasionally a man

67

may open a chest and a mouse may scuttle into it without his realizing it. If the garment was damaged by moths, then one must consider whether or not the purchaser had the garment long enough for the damage to have occurred while he was in possession: If the time of his possession was brief, the damage clearly occurred while the vendor was in possession. If the time of his possession was long enough so that the moth damage *could* have occurred during the purchaser's time of possession, the sale is not rescinded. This matter is to be resolved on the basis of the specific circumstances: we find in *B. Hullin* 51a and *B. Kethuboth* 76b[1] that we make distinctions concerning a metal object which has pierced the second stomach of a ritually slaughtered cow. There the case is that a butcher purchased the cow, slaughtered it, and found, upon dressing the carcass, that an internal organ was damaged in such a fashion as to render the beast unfit for consumption by Jews. The animal found to be so marred represents a loss for the butcher who had wished to make a profit on it. The Talmud makes the following distinction: If the internal wound had begun to scab, then it is presumed that the wound was made at least three days before the slaughter. The animal was therefore purchased under a mistake of fact and the sale can be rescinded; after all, the butcher had paid good money for a healthy meat animal. If the internal wound had not scabbed over, there is a doubt as to when the injury occurred and the butcher must then prove that the animal was injured prior to his purchase of it. (Thus we have it that the nature of a given sort of damage may be affected by a specific period of time—before or after three days prior to the slaughter.) . . .

In my humble opinion, I would say that moth damage would require thirty days. This is derived from the talmudic remarks concerning a piece of found property, e.g., a woolen garment—which one takes care of by shaking it out once every thirty days, so that the item may eventually be restored undamaged to its owner, *B. Bava Mezia* 29b. If it were possible in this case that the moths could devour it in less than thirty days, they would allow (the purchaser) a correspondingly shorter period (of grace in which moth damage is presumed to exist prior to his possession). One must also take into consideration whether the garment was kept spread out or stored away, and whether it was a rainy season or a dry one. Everything in this area is to be determined by the opinion of experts who possess refined religious scruples. If there is any doubt in the matter, the claimant who wishes reimbursement must prove why he is entitled to it.

Rabbenu Asher rendered a decision in a responsum[2] about a man who purchased a cheese. When he opened the cheese three days later, he found a huge mass of rot. Rabbenu Asher asserted that if it is the expert opinion of cheese makers that a mass of rot like this could not have developed in only three days the sale can be rescinded: it was done under a mistake of fact. If there was doubt about the matter, the purchaser-claimant has to bring proof why the sale could be rescinded. This is also cited in *Tur, Hoshen Mishpat* 232. If the garment has already been tailored and he wore it before the damage was noticed, and the damage was of a sort that would not appear before now, the garment is returned to the seller—by one of the aforementioned procedures—and the seller has to refund the price of the clothing. This is what Maimonides wrote in *Hilkhoth Mekhirah,* chap. 16, in regard to one who sold a building which was later found to be defective. If (the vendor) had repaired the garment and restored some of its value, one reckons the cost of repair and a fee for his wearing of it and (the vendor) pays him the balance. (Presumably the sale is rescinded, but the full purchase price is not refunded; the garment, after all, was *not* a total loss.)

This is my humble opinion. (Signed) Solomon b. R. Simon b. Zemah.

## Notes and References

1. Maimonides, *Hilkhoth Mekhirah* 17:4, 20:15; cf. also *B. Bava Bathra* 96a.
2. Responsum no. 102:9.

See also *Shulhan Arukh, Hoshen Mishpat* 232:3, 13; Benjamin Rabinowitz-Teomim, *Hukkat Mishpat*, cols. 90 ff.; Gulak, *Yesode Hamishpat Haivri*, vol. 1, pp. 63 ff.; Herzog, *Main Institutions of Jewish Law*; cf. also R. Meir of Rothenburg's case, No. 258.

# R. Solomon b. Simon Duran

No. 16    Usury

*Decision:* A vendor who sold goods on credit, which goods fell in value to half their price, so that the purchaser could not pay the cash price and instead returned an amount of goods to the vendor, is not a usurer by reason of a demand for an additional cash sum to make up the full price of the goods. The payment of a full price does not constitute usury even if the goods have fallen in price.

---

*You asked further:* Reuben purchased from Simon a quantity of merchandise at one dinar per pound. He transported the goods to his city. The transaction was on credit. After some time Simon came for payment. Reuben did not have the money to pay. Reuben paid Simon the same quantity of goods of the same sort, which had fallen in price to one-half dinar per pound. Simon wants the rest of his money. Reuben says: "You have no claim against me. The goods I took from you at a high price, you have gotten from me at a low price. This is usury!" (That is, for Reuben to give Simon a quantity of goods or cash to cover the decline in the price would surely be unjustifiable and usurious profit for Simon!) Simon pleads: "The goods you purchased from me were sold to you at the then going rate. If they fell in price afterwards, the price drop is your responsibility. Moreover, you already sold my merchandise (presumably at a loss)—this merchandise offered in return is *other* merchandise."

*Answer:* If the original selling price was not the market price, but rather Simon increased the price since that price had not yet been paid (i.e., an additional charge for credit, the additional charge) should (not) be collected. Whatever increase Simon made in the price—irrespective of any later price fluctuation, since the going rate for the goods was public knowledge, provided he did in fact raise the price of the goods over the going rate—is indirect interest (an unlawful usurious gain, but not a

70

specific return on a loan as such, which constitutes unqualified, biblical interest). Since the price has not yet been paid, Reuben may lawfully retain possession of the additional charge for credit.

However, if the sale was made at the established going rate, even though someone may sell the commodity for less in the marketplace, there is no element of usury, for there is much that goes on between "sell to me" and "buy from me" (i.e., the established price may well be affected by individuals bargaining with each other). How much the more (is there no element of usury) if the purchase was made at the time of the higher price—which was current among merchants—and *afterwards* the price dropped. (Gains and losses were not due to the manipulation of the parties, but to the forces of the marketplace.)

Even if Simon repurchased the very same goods from Reuben, the transaction is permissible, because Reuben had (earlier) effected a formal and legal sale (and had acquired the goods by sale so that no element of loan existed, despite the fact that the *price* was not yet paid. Therefore even if Simon repurchased the very same goods at a lower price, so that he would have the goods for less—there would be no element of usury). This concept is present in the Talmud (*B. Bava Mezia* 63a): That the effecting of a formal transfer rules out usury in several transactions involving credit that might appear to be usurious. The sages did not prohibit transactions that look suspicious except when there is clear intent to evade the laws against usury. Thus *B. Bava Mezia* 62b: "There are some transactions which are lawful but nonetheless prohibited because they are done with the clear intent of evading the laws against usury. How is this? If A said, lend me one hundred *zuzim,* and B said, I have no cash but I shall give you one hundred *zuzim* worth of wheat, and B gave the one hundred *zuzim* of wheat but then repurchased the wheat for ninety *zuzim,* the transaction is unlawful because it is a clear evasion of the law against interest. (B had gotten one hundred *zuzim* worth for ninety, profiting on his money. Or, the original request for a loan of one hundred is discounted ten percent; B, the creditor, in effect gets ten percent of the gross for his cash.) The matter indicates by its substance that it was only prohibited when done with the intent to evade the laws against usury.

However, in the case under notice, where Reuben purchased goods at the going rate, and they fell in price later (by market forces, not Simon's manipulation), and Simon collected his merchandise from him as payment on the debt, such merchandise being worth half its original price, (a claim for the balance of the price) is not usury or an unlawful tactic to evade usury.

71

(The creditor, B, got one hundred for ninety because he rigged the loan and the sale. Simon sold at, e.g., one hundred. He did not manipulate the price. His acceptance of that same one hundred worth of goods, at a current value of fifty, does not put Simon into the position of B, who repurchased to his advantage. If he had given Reuben one hundred worth and then took back that same one hundred worth for, e.g., an arbitrary eighty, then Reuben as a debtor would be paying interest indirectly because of the discount on the purchase price. However, Simon is *not* regaining one hundred worth at a fraction of that value. He is really only getting fifty worth because of the price drop. The fact that Simon takes back "one hundred" valued at fifty is misleading; the return of high-priced goods when their value has declined is no advantage to the creditor. It is not as if he had himself loaned at one value and *bought* back at an artificially low price, discounting the sale as a device for forcing a debtor in effect to pay interest. Reuben, of course, would argue, unsuccessfully, that now Simon has "one hundred" worth, which he, Reuben, would have to sell off [even to Simon] at a fraction of his cost, and certainly a payment for price differential is illegal!)

## Notes and References

On the evasion of interest, see *Encyclopedia Talmudit,* vol. 9, col. 714. Cf. also Haim Cohn's article "Usury," *E.J.,* vol. 16, cols. 27-33.

# R. Solomon b. Simon Duran

**No. 241**    Goods damaged in transit

*Decision:* A carrier is liable for damage, due to his negligence, to goods in transit.

---

*You asked further:* Reuben shipped a consignment of colored and white woolen garments with Simon. Simon transported them from one city to another. Simon packed all the garments together and loaded them on one of his two pack animals. While Simon was en route, he came to a river. He took the harness of the lead animal and led it across the river. There was no incident or accident in the crossing. When he reached his destination, he discovered that the dyestuff on the colored garments had run onto the white garments. Simon pleads that he did not know on which animal the white goods had been loaded. What is the law on this? Is Simon liable to pay damages or not?

*Answer:* It appears to me that if this bailee (Simon is treated as a bailee, entrusted with the goods) knew the white goods were on the second animal, he is liable for damages—even if he were unpaid for his service as a bailee. All bailees are held liable for their negligence! This is set forth in the Talmud, *B. Bava Mezia* 82b. The bailee in this case did not exercise the standard of care reasonably expected on his part. According to the inquiry, Simon was already somewhat apprehensive about the first animal which he took to the river to cool off. When he did this he left the second animal unattended. If he knew that the white goods were on the second, unattended animal, he was negligent. . . .

Similarly: If the dyed garments were of such a nature that, when the animal got into the water, the dyestuff would run, and he did not wrap the white goods sufficiently to protect them from the colored goods, he was negligent. Even if, when the animal eventually got into the water, it did so in an accident which Simon was powerless to prevent, e.g., it bucked and ran and Simon could not bring it back under control and

73

*then* the water caused the colors to run on the white garment—even here, Simon is liable for damages. The Talmud, *B. Bava Mezia* 42a, asserts that although the immediate cause of loss may be a catastrophic accident, if an original element of negligence clearly was a contributing factor in the loss, the bailee is held liable nonetheless.* However, if Simon did *not* know that the white garment was on the second, un-attended animal, he is not liable for water damage. But, if the dye ran because of the animal's sweat or there was damage due to the heat of the sun (e.g., fading), Simon is liable from any point of view. The indemnity he must pay is that which the court will determine: they assess how much the damage has affected the value of the item; the claimant keeps his damaged item, and the bailee pays the difference between the value of the property when undamaged and the value of the property when damaged, cf. *B. Bava Qamma* 11a.

## Notes and References

* Cf. *B. Bava Mezia* 42a; Maimonides, *Hilkhoth Sekhiruth* 1:4; *Hilkhoth She'elah Ufikadon* 4:6.
    See also Maimonides, *Hilkhoth Sheluhim* 2:9; *Tur, Shulhan Arukh, Hoshen Mishpat* 187.

# R. Meir b. Baruch of Rothenburg

**No. 251**    Property rescued from a fire

---

*Decision:* An article rescued from a fire, it clearly being the case that the owners of the article have abandoned the article, becomes lawful property of the rescuer.

---

*You asked* concerning the fire that broke out in a town and spread so rapidly that people fled the town out of fear of this fire. One Jew stayed long enough to save a book, the owners of which had fled. (The question is, of course, who owns the rescued volume?)

*Answer:* He is not obliged to return it to the (former) owners, because he (the new owner) may claim, "I took possession of it when it was ownerless, abandoned property." This is in line with the talmudic discussion, *B. Bava Qamma* 115a. There, the following case is presented: One person is carrying a cask of wine along the road; another is carrying a cask of honey, which is a more costly commodity. The cask of honey breaks and the honey begins to spill out; thereupon the man with the case of wine pours out his wine and uses his cask to catch the dripping honey. The rule is that the man saving the honey is entitled only to as much of it (the honey) as would cover payment for his exertion, not to all of it. Yet, is he not able to claim that the honey he saved was in fact "ownerless," since it would have been a total loss without his efforts? The Talmud relates a rule demonstrating that produce subject to tithe and, in imminent danger of being lost or destroyed, cannot on the spot be designated as the requisite tithes, etc., in respect to similar produce safe in the owner's house. This is so because the goods are in imminent danger and become "ownerless." It follows that the man cannot declare them to be his tithe, etc. If he should make such a declaration, it is a nullity. The Talmud rejoins that the honey in the case under notice does not become ownerless because the cask in question is understood to be encased in a bale of twigs used for holding olives to be pressed. Therefore the honey is not in immediate danger of utter destruction. Were this not the case, then indeed the man saving the honey could claim the whole of its value because it was indeed ownerless*. . . . (Signed) Meir b. Baruch.

## Notes and References

* For further information, cf. *Shulhan Arukh, Hoshen Mishpat* 264:5, gloss; Menahem Elon's article, "Hazakah," *E.J.*, vol. 7, cols. 1516-22.
    See also Wahrhaftig, *Hahazakah Bamishpat Haivri*, pp. 129 ff.; *Encyclopedia Talmudit*, vol. 10, cols. 50 ff., esp. col. 92.